TOPICS IN APPLIED GEOGRAPHY

GLACIER HAZARDS

TOPICS IN APPLIED GEOGRAPHY
edited by Donald Davidson and John Dawson

Lance Tufnell
The Polytechnic
Huddersfield

GLACIER HAZARDS

Longman
London
and New York

Longman Group Limited
Longman House, Burnt Mill, Harlow
Essex CM20 2JE, England
Associated companies throughout the world

*Published in the United States of America
by Longman Inc., New York*

First published 1984

British Library Cataloguing in Publication Data
Tufnell, Lance
   Glacier hazards. – (Topics in applied geography)
   1. Glaciers
   I. Title
   551.3'12   QE576

   ISBN 0-582-30065-7

Library of Congress Cataloging in Publication Data
Tufnell, Lance, 1940–
   Glacier hazards.

   (Topics in applied geography)
   Bibliography: p.
   Includes index. .
   1. Glaciers.   2. Hazardous geographic environments.
   I. Title.   II. Series.
   GB2405.T83   1982   551.3'12   82-23960
   ISBN 0-582-30065-7

Set in 9/11 pt Times Roman
Printed in Singapore by
Selector Printing Co (Pte) Ltd

CONTENTS

LIST OF FIGURES

LIST OF TABLES

LIST OF PLATES

ACKNOWLEDGEMENTS

We are grateful to the following for permission to reproduce copyright materials:

A. A. Balkema and the authors for our Fig 2.1 after F. Roethlisberger and W. Schneebeli (1979); Bókaútgáfa Menningarsjóds for our Figs 3.2 and 4.2 after S. Thorarinsson (1956); Bolletino Comitato Glaciologico Italiano for our Fig 2.2 after S. Belloni (1970); David & Charles for our Table 2.2 after D. H. S. Richardson (1975); the Editor, *Die Alpen* and the authors for our Figs 6.3 and 6.4 after F. Röthlisberger and W. Schneebeli (1976); Geographica Helvetica and the author for our Fig 2.3 after F. Röthlisberger (1980); Hallwag Publishers and Editions Payot for our Fig 4.3 after R. C. Bachmann (1979); La Houille Blanche for our Table 6.6 after P. Kasser and M. Aellen (1976); International Association of Hydrological Sciences for our Table 5.1 after B. Morales (1966); IAHS and UNESCO for our Tables 6.4 and 6.5 after F. Müller (1977); La Murithienne for our Fig 6.2 after D. Aubert (1980). Table 6.1 after I. Mariētan (1955) and Tables 6.2 and 6.3 after A. Bezinge and G. Bonvin (1974); National Research Council of Canada for our Fig 5.1 after H. C. Hoinkes (1969); Regents of the University of Colorado, the Editor, *Zeitschrift für Gletscherkunde und Glazialgeologie* and the author for our Fig 2.4 after B. Messerli (1975, 1978); the author, Dr Hans Röthlisberger for our Fig 7.1 after H. Röthlisberger (1974); UNESCO, WMO and IAHS for our Table 4.1 after G. Østrem (1972); the Editor, *Water Power and Dam Construction* for our Fig 4.1 after R. Partl (1978); the Editor, *Zeitschrift für Gletscherkunde und Glazialgeologie* for our Fig 5.2 after W. Welsch and H. Kinzl (1970).

CHAPTER 1
THE PROBLEM IN PERSPECTIVE

Environmental hazards constitute a world problem of growing importance. Those due to natural processes are alone thought to be costing mankind tens of billions of dollars a year. While the damage they cause to property is mainly sustained by the industrialized countries, the loss of life, which averages 250,000 people a year, is chiefly borne by the poorer nations. Much of this destruction and death is the result of climatic events, particularly floods, tropical cyclones and drought (Kates 1980). Also very troublesome is the principal non-climatic hazard, earthquakes. There is in addition a rather less significant group of hazardous processes which includes volcanic activity, snow avalanches, landslides and frost. Together these two sets of processes have provided the main topics for discussion in a number of books on natural hazards (e.g. Coates 1971: Castiglioni 1974; White 1974; Bolt *et al*. 1975). However, in only one of these (Castiglioni) is there an important section on glacier hazards. The reasons for this are probably twofold:

1. Glaciers are at present in a contracted state and most do not appear particularly threatening. People may therefore know something of, for example, the dangers posed by crevasses, but have little appreciation of those more important hazards which are due to glacier fluctuations. Yet, were there to be even a small climatic deterioration, those same glaciers would expand, as they have on several previous occasions, and would become more hazardous to mankind. By dealing chiefly with occurrences of the last 100 years, recent books on natural hazards have usually failed to appreciate that the present relatively low level of glacier nuisance merely constitutes a lull between the more hazardous events of the Little Ice Age (1550–1860) and those of some future period of climatic deterioration.

2. Academic curricula often pay little attention to the study of how glacier fluctuations have affected mankind. In Britain, for example, most emphasis is usually placed on an examination of glacial geomorphology and, tc a lesser extent, glaciology. By contrast, glacier hazards are largely ignored, so there is little appreciation of the subject among students and little demand for information about it. Teaching establishments must therefore develop curricula which accurately reflect the human significance of glacier fluctuations. This in turn will encourage authors to include the subject in their books on natural hazards.

Because of the present situation, the chapters which follow aim to demonstrate that glacier–man relationships are worth serious and detailed consideration. Although no one would claim that the topic represents a major branch of hazard studies, its importance has clearly been underestimated in the past.

The best-known glacier dangers are those which may afflict climbers and skiers.

They include the problems due to hidden crevasses and falling ice. Less widely appreciated, but of potentially greater importance, is the build-up of atmospheric carbon dioxide and the possible effects of this on glacier melting and sea-level. It is not, however, the object of the present book to discuss either of these topics, significant though they may be. Instead, attention is confined to hazards posed by small-scale glacier fluctuations of the type which has characterized the historic period. When climate has deteriorated in places such as the Alps and Iceland, glaciers have expanded, thereby threatening or even overrunning settlements, agricultural land, communications and other manifestations of human activity. Small-scale glacier fluctuations are also critical for the supply of meltwater which has traditionally been used for drinking and irrigation, but which has more recently become important for the development of hydroelectricity. In addition, these fluctuations can affect the incidence of glacier floods and ice avalanches, both of which are violent hazards with the ability to take life as well as to destroy property (Fig. 1.1). The dangers caused by historical glacier fluctuations are first examined in general terms (Chs 3–5). They are then discussed with reference to a specific area, the canton of Valais in southern Switzerland (Chs 6–8). This area was chosen for special study because its glaciers are easily accessible to a large number of Europeans who may be interested in the problem and because it has witnessed a long and fairly well-documented encounter between glaciers and man. Undertaking a small-area study has also allowed discussion of the glacier problem to be extended through a consideration of man's responses to the hazard within the canton and an examination of possible scenarios for its future. This latter topic is fraught with difficulties and has therefore been kept relatively simple (Ch. 8). To have discussed adequately contentious issues such as the 'snowblitz' theory of glaciation or the effects on glaciers and sea-level of the man-induced build-up of atmospheric carbon dioxide would have meant lengthening the book significantly through the inclusion of much speculative material of uncertain value. Hence, the present book treats glacier fluctuations as part of an essentially natural system which is largely controlled by slow-moving atmospheric changes. This does not imply a firm rejection of the 'snowblitz' idea nor is it meant to deny the possibility that in the future variations of the system might become more strongly influenced, directly or indirectly, by human activity.

Information on glacier fluctuations and the resultant hazards is scattered throughout a variety of sources, many of which are not in English. With very few exceptions, there has been little attempt to gather this disparate material into a coherent overview. Perhaps the most important contribution to the subject is a book by Emmanuel le Roy Ladurie which appeared in French under the title *Histoire du climat depuis l'an mil* and was later revised and translated into English as *Times of feast, times of famine: a history of climate since the year 1000* (Ladurie 1967, 1972). However, as their titles indicate, these books cover a field wider than the study of glacier variations and hazards. Moreover, Ladurie tells the glacier story in an essentially chronological and minutely detailed fashion, which makes it difficult, particularly for those who are new to the subject, to extract the main threads of his argument. The present book bases itself on what are regarded as the subject's main themes and thereby consigns the detail to a supportive and underlining role. In addition, it covers aspects of the subject which received little or no attention from Ladurie: these include data sources for elucidating the story of historical glacier fluctuations, human response to the glacier hazard problem and speculation about future trends. It is gratifying to note that data on glacier hazards also appear in some of the most recent books. For example, there are a number of paragraphs on the topic scattered throughout Bach-

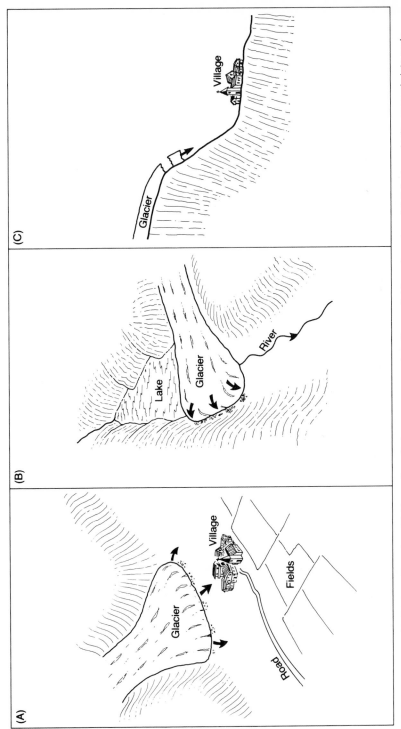

Fig 1.1 Three types of glacier hazard.   (A) Expanding glacier overruns nearby villages, fields and roads.   (B) Tributary glacier expands into main valley, blocks river and forms lake. Glacier dam eventually gives way and destructive flood results.   (C) Ice breaks from snout of glacier, avalanches into valley and destroys objects in its path.

mann's *Glaciers des Alpes* (Bachmann 1979), while a more substantial account is found in *Les glaciers sont vivants* by Vivian (1979). Even so, these books give only limited coverage of the glacier hazard problem and largely restrict their examples to the European Alps. Though this is the classic area for the subject and is therefore frequently mentioned in the present book, some glacier hazards (e.g. *débâcles*) have developed better elsewhere.

If glacier fluctuations are to constitute a hazard, they must have contact with people and property or they must at least appear threatening. According to Lliboutry (1971), glaciers cover 16,300,000 km² of the earth's surface, but only 10,000–20,000 of this total lies near inhabited areas. However, this figure is unlikely to remain static, as glacier–man relationships are constantly changing.

For their part, glaciers can pose different problems at different times as illustrated by the experience of Le Tour, a village near the head of the Chamonix valley in the French Alps. When glaciers expanded during the Little Ice Age, this village was more than once almost overrun by ice. Since then the offending Le Tour glacier has retreated away from the village, so that its present terminus lies near the top of a cliff. The danger now is that ice might break away from the glacier and avalanche towards the village (see also Chs 3 and 5). Although this example demonstrates that both advancing and retreating glaciers can prove hazardous, it is the former that tend to create the most problems. Grove (1972), using Norwegian examples, was therefore able to show that damage caused by glaciers and other natural hazards increased during the more severe phases of the Little Ice Age.

Glacier–man relationships are also influenced by the modern tendency to push settlement and economic development ever closer to the limits of the habitable world. Thus, various kinds of human activity are still being undertaken within historic glacier limits: sometimes this means the creation of fresh hazards, while on other occasions it merely serves to replace existing dangers by new ones (for examples, see Chs 6 and 7). Technology and science are now playing an increasing role in man's efforts to protect himself against glacier hazards. Unfortunately, as with other natural hazards, there will always be a gap between what is technologically possible and that which is worthwhile protecting on the basis of economic expediency and human needs. It will therefore probably never happen that all places become protected from all types of glacier hazard on all occasions. Finally, the timing of a glacier event may affect the impact it has on man. An example would be the 1965 ice avalanche at Mattmark (Valais) which struck as workmen were changing shifts and were therefore at the site in twice their usual numbers (Chs 6 and 7).

The shifting relationships between glaciers and man are continually altering the extent to which people and property suffer from the hazard. As already mentioned, the present contracted state of glaciers is responsible for a level of nuisance below that of some historical periods. It may, however, be that climatic deterioration since the 1940s heralds a new phase of glacier expansion. If this is so, any structure built within historic glacier limits is at risk in the same way that medieval settlements and cultivation were threatened following the onset of climatic decline in the thirteenth century. Our greater understanding of glacier behaviour should, of course, help us avoid mistakes similar to those perpetrated by the medieval settlers and farmers, but this has not always happened. Consequently, it is to be hoped that modern planners will increase their awareness of the problems which can arise due to glacier fluctuations and will translate that awareness into meaningful planning decisions. The importance of this point can be underlined by distinguishing between *actual* and *potential* hazards. Included in the first category would be those natural processes which currently have an adverse impact on people and property: the second group would consist of processes whose dangerous effects are at present minimal, but which might in future show a pronounced upsurge due either to variations in environmental processes (e.g. climatic changes) or to human activity (e.g. new engineering work). Such a distinction does not exclude the possibility that a given type of natural process might be an actual hazard in one place, but only a potential hazard in another. It similarly allows for the fact that in a particular locality a natural process may create an actual hazard during one period, but only a potential hazard during another. Clearly, many glaciers are at present a potential, rather than an actual hazard.

The literature has often treated natural hazards as if they were part of a fundamentally static system and has consequently underplayed the variable nature of the dangers they can present. Both scientists and planners therefore need to appreciate that a natural process which is of little importance to man at present might have the potential to become far more dangerous in the future.

CHAPTER 2
ESTABLISHING THE NATURE OF GLACIER FLUCTUATIONS

A STORY OF GROWING COMPLEXITY

The greater our efforts to understand Earth history, the more complex is the story we uncover. It has therefore become necessary to regard the Earth as an immensely varied and forever changing planet. This view has gained much support from investigations of climatic and glacial history. Accepted opinion used to see glaciation as an environmental anomaly which had occurred during perhaps 0.5 per cent of geological time and which thereby merited the Davisian label 'climatic accident' (Dury 1960). Now, however, people think of glacial periods as a more common feature of Earth history. It is no longer possible, for example, to regard the Pleistocene as having begun only 1 million years ago with the onset of widespread glaciation (see Holmes 1965). Instead, the Plio-Pleistocene boundary has been pushed back another 1–2 million years and the Tertiary has become a period when glaciation was not uncommon. Thus, Tricart (1970) has pointed out that Eocene morainic deposits occur in the Rocky Mountains, while Sugden (1978) has claimed that the build-up of Antarctic ice started in Oligocene/mid Miocene times.

Modern research has also changed our views on the complexity of Pleistocene events. The classic sequence of four glaciations (Günz, Mindel, Riss, Würm) put forward early this century by Penck and Brückner in Alpine Europe and often taken as the model for establishing Pleistocene successions elsewhere, is now being supplanted by a more detailed and varied picture. According to this the number of Pleistocene glacials has been far higher than was previously thought – Gribbin (1976) and Bowen (1977), for example, have claimed that twenty or more can be identified. Although the exact status of recently discovered 'glacial' periods may well be unclear, their identification nevertheless strengthens the belief that Pleistocene environments have been very varied and changeable. Of perhaps greater importance for mankind are some of the newer ideas about the speed with which glaciations can begin. Older theories proposed that major glaciations developed over thousands of years and were characterized by slow temperature decline, a gradual accumulation of ice, especially in mountain areas, and the unhurried movement of that ice towards adjacent lowlands. Ideas developed around 1970 by Lamb and Woodroffe suggest an alternative possibility whereby glaciation may become established within 100 years, due to the incomplete melting of consecutive winter snows. Under such conditions, glaciers would quickly form, as it were, 'from below'. Owing to this rapid development, the phenomenon has been called a 'snowblitz' (Calder 1974; Gribbin 1976). Were it ever to become reality, the consequences for mankind would obviously be catastrophic.

Complexity of the Pleistocene is further increased by the fact that the major glacial and interglacial periods can be subdivided. Thus, the waning phases of the last (Devensian) glacial, together with the 10,000 or so years of the Holocene (Flandrian), can be subdivided into about 10 periods, each with its own characteristics. The present one began some 2,500 years ago and is generally known as the 'Sub-Atlantic'. Although it can be described as a time of cool, moist climate in an area such as western Europe, there have been a number of recognizable variations. For example, the changes of the last 1,000 years make it possible to identify four distinctive periods and perhaps the beginnings of a fifth (Table 2.1). The differences between these periods have, of course, been small, as illustrated by the fact that from the mid nineteenth to the mid twentieth centuries mean annual temperatures increased only by around 1 °C. Nevertheless, minor changes of this sort can often have significant effects on human activity. Particularly important for the present book is the way in which small

Table 2.1 Climatic changes since AD 1000 (summarized from Lamb 1974, 1977)

PERIOD	CHARACTERISTICS
Since about 1940	Irregular temperature decline. Cooling most pronounced in high latitudes. Some glacier regeneration. Droughts widespread, especially between 10 ° and 30 °N. Precipitation increases markedly in certain other regions (e.g. some high-latitude areas)
Modern climatic improvement	Peak warmth achieved in the 1930s/1940s when temperatures approached those of the medieval optimum. Widespread disappearance of sea ice, glaciers and permafrost. Many localities had maximum precipitation averages in the first half of the twentieth century, though places in the rain shadow of the Rockies and Andes became drier. Period terminated first in higher latitudes
Little Ice Age	Generally harsh climate within which there were times of increased severity (e.g. *c.* 1600). The beginnings and end of the period were not contemporaneous everywhere. Glaciers and other cold climate phenomena in an expanded and active state
Decline into the Little Ice Age	Began earlier in northerly latitudes than further south, where, however, it was preceded by a time of increased storminess (e.g. around North Sea coasts). Ice increased in northern waters; temperatures declined; glaciers and permafrost expanded; the tree-line fell. Westerly winds became stronger and more prevalent, so moisture was transported more successfully into Eurasia. In North America the Rockies acted as a barrier to westerly winds and rain shadow areas became drier
Medieval warm period (Little Optimum)	The period of peak warmth was not contemporaneous everywhere (e.g. it occurred earlier in inland North America and Greenland than over most of Europe). In many areas temperatures approached those of the Holocene optimum, with the warmest month 0.5–1.5 °C above 1900 levels in western Europe. Until about 1200 many places had a climate moister than that of the present, but thereafter some areas (e.g. parts of the USA) became drier

climatic changes are 'magnified' when translated into glacier fluctuations (Ladurie 1967, 1972).

The great problem which needs to be solved, is how to predict the dangers resulting from glacier fluctuations in the near future. An accurate evaluation of this hazard partly rests on being able to assess the status of the last 10,000 or so years. In discussing this period, some authors have used rather non-committal terms, like 'Holocene' and 'Flandrian'. Others have preferred more loaded words, such as 'post-glacial' and 'interglacial', though it is arguable that these are misleading, for snow and ice continue to be widespread on Earth. During northern-hemisphere winters, they cover half of the world's land area and nearly one-third of its oceans. Moreover, of the four major Devensian ice sheets, only two (those of Eurasia and North America) have so far disappeared (Sugden 1978). Consequently, the Earth is neither in a post- nor interglacial period, but still experiences widespread glacierization. Also relevant to predictions of the ice threat are views about the length of the so-called 'interglacials'. Under the classic Penck–Brückner scheme these are allotted rather long spans of time. In particular, the Mindel–Riss ('Great') interglacial was supposed to have been of considerable duration, having persisted for about 310,000 years. Some modern writers, however, think that interglacials were much shorter, lasting for only 10,000–12,000 years (Gribbin 1976; Bryson and Murray 1977). If this is true, there are enormous implications for mankind, since the Holocene began 10,200 years ago. Consequently, there are those who predict another major glaciation within 2,000 years and yet others who believe that such a period is being delayed only through warming of the atmosphere by human activities. On the other hand, there are still people who consider that the next glaciation is much further away – perhaps 10,000 years, according to Lamb (1974).

Opinions about the seriousness of the ice threat may also be influenced by personal experiences of climatic events. Twentieth-century scientists, especially those who remember the inter-war years, may be prone to over-optimistic forecasts, unless they give full cognizance to the fact that the climate of recent decades has not been typical of that experienced during the previous 1,000 years and has been even more unlike that of the past 1 million years (Bryson and Murray 1977). Only by acquiring detailed and accurate knowledge of climatic trends over fairly long periods can our own experiences be put into perspective.

ESTABLISHING THE NATURE OF GLACIER FLUCTUATIONS DURING HISTORIC TIMES

A clear understanding of historic glacier fluctuations can only be obtained by drawing upon the approaches and techniques of several different subjects. The point is under-lined by the excellent work of Messerli and collaborators (1975, 1978) who studied historical variations of the Grindelwald glaciers. This kind of multidisciplinary approach is needed partly because individual data types often give an incomplete picture of glacier fluctuations and also because the cross-checking of observations from different sources helps to identify errors. Much information on historical glacier variations has to be collected through field-work, though enough documentary evidence has now been accumulated for second-hand investigations to represent a valuable field of inquiry. Our uneven knowledge of recent glacial behaviour in different areas of the world is partly a function of research effort, but it also stems from the availability of evidence. For example, written data are more abundant for the European glaciers than for those of the Karakoram. Similarly, tephrochronolo-gical work can be undertaken only in a limited number of places (e.g. Iceland).

Landforms and deposits

Moraines have long been regarded as valuable indicators of former glacial limits. The terminal (end) variety in particular has been widely used for this purpose (Porter 1981). Lateral moraines can also help in the defining of ice margins and in calculating the amounts of downwasting which have occurred since their formation. Even where morainic material does not give rise to distinctive landscape features, its extent can still be mapped in an attempt to locate former glacial boundaries.

Although the technique of using moraines for the field identification of previous ice limits appears straightforward in outline, it often encounters difficulties when applied in detail to real-world situations. Part of the problem is that there have been too few scientific observations of moraine development, largely because most glaciers have been contracting in recent decades An exception is the work of Rabassa, Rubulis and Suárez (1979), who observed push-moraine formation by the Frias glacier (Argentina) during 1976–78. They noted, for example, that in 1977 moraines rose 2.5 m above their surroundings following a 38 m advance of ice during the previous twelve months. This kind of work needs to become more common, if our understanding of moraines as indicators of former glacial limits is to improve. Such features in fact provide an essentially discontinuous record of glacier fluctuations and are therefore difficult to use for the temporal and spatial delimitation of recession between periods of moraine building (Porter 1981).

There is also a need to increase our knowledge of how well moraines can survive attack by denudational processes. On the one hand, the absence of such features cannot automatically be taken as proof that they have never existed in an area. Thus, in Iceland, many glaciers reached or were very close to their historic maximum as late as the 1880s and it is only from then onwards that moraines are available for working out variations in ice cover (Thorarinsson 1943). On the other hand, some end moraines clearly do not indicate the limits of glacier expansion, for although essentially intact, they have been at least once overridden by ice. Examples of this have been described by Karlén (1973) who worked in the Kebnekaise Mountains, Swedish Lapland. Using photographs taken at various times during the twentieth century, he has demonstrated that some glaciers in this region advanced over pre-existing moraine ridges, before later contracting to expose them again.

Further problems arise because there are some features which look like moraines, but which are, in fact, of a non-glacial origin (Porter 1981). T. G. Bonney (1902) has described a number of nineteenth-century events from the Alps and elsewhere which demonstrate that the material laid down by swollen torrents can closely resemble moraine.

The dating of moraines and corresponding ice limits has also met with difficulties. Certainly, there have been too many occasions when research workers have merely assumed an age for a particular moraine or have based their dating on some vague criterion, such as a 'fresh' or 'degraded' appearance. Recently, however, it has been shown that lateral moraines in the Alps, which were often attributed to Little Ice Age processes, have been built up over a much longer period (Röthlisberger 1976; Roethlisberger and Schneebeli 1979: Röthlisberger *et al.* 1980). This discovery originated in particular from an examination of fossil soils which can occur at several different levels within a lateral moraine (Fig. 2.1A). Carbon$_{14}$ dating of these soils enables the history of moraine formation to be unravelled. The fossil soil content of glacial moraines in the western Alps has also been studied by Müller (1975) and Schneebeli (1976).

Alpine research has used solifluction lobes for the dating of some moraines. These

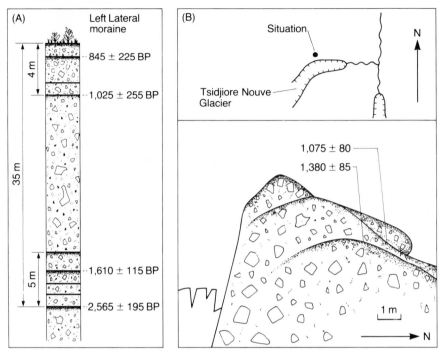

Fig 2.1   A and B   The position and age of fossil soils in the moraines of (A) the Findel and (B) the Tsidjiore Nouve glaciers, Valais. (After Roethlisberger and Schneebeli, 1979).

tend to be located on the outer slopes of moraines and have fossil soils on their upper surfaces. Dating the soils gives a minimum age for the underlying moraine and helps to identify times of relative warmth (Röthlisberger 1976; Roethlisberger and Schneebeli 1979) (Fig. 2.1B). In a similar way, tephra horizons within moraines can be used for dating, especially if they are closely spaced and providing their ages are known (Porter 1981). By examining such horizons it has, for example, been possible to show that the greatest Holocene expansion of Brúarjökull occurred as recently as 1890 (Thorarinsson 1964). Although this and other geomorphological studies have yielded valuable data about ice limits in the historic period and earlier, there is often a need to widen the scope of inquiry by using vegetation-based techniques such as lichenometry and dendroglaciology.

Vegetation

Of several techniques which use vegetation to study recent glacier fluctuations, the most popular is lichenometry, a subject pioneered by the Austrian botanist, Roland Beschel. His early paper *Flechten als Altersmasstab rezenter Moränen* (published 1950) has now been translated into English (Beschel 1973) and represents a landmark in the subject's history. Particularly during the last ten years, the application of lichenometry to glacial studies has developed rapidly, though there are still places where it has been surprisingly little used (e.g. the French Alps: Vivian 1979). Unfortunately, the techniques of lichenometry continue to be plagued with difficulties, so that the data they provide should be treated with caution (Innes 1981).

The study of glacier fluctuations using lichenometry is based on a mixture of facts and assumptions. They include:

1. Lichens are among the first plants to colonize an area soon after it has been vacated by a retreating glacier. They can therefore be used to obtain an approximate measure of the time since the ice disappeared. Although these assumptions generally hold true, there are exceptions. For example, lichen colonization does not always immediately follow the disappearance of an ice cover. Thus, an area deglaciated around 1914 by the Russell glacier (Alaska) was only partly colonized by *Rhizocarpon geographicum* nearly sixty years later. It has also been found that numerous moraines in the region have had their surfaces disturbed by the melting of internal ice and by downslope movements. Consequently, lichen diameters do not give an accurate indication of when the moraines first stabilized. In addition, many of the area's moraines have been vegetation covered, so that rock surfaces became overgrown and lichen development was interrupted. Similarly, a number of moraines formed 1,100 C_{14} years ago consist largely of volcanic ash, which is easily redistributed by wind and may thus have periodically covered lichens growing on rock surfaces. Hence, specimens now found there are not an accurate pointer to moraine age (Denton and Karlén 1973). Elsewhere (e.g. on Baffin Island) lichens appear to have survived beneath an ice cover and so do not provide a reliable indication of when this last retreated from the area (Falconer 1966).

2. Although lichen growth rates are basically slow, they do exhibit variations (Table 2.2). For example, in the high Arctic they tend to be less than in maritime mid-latitude mountain ranges. Hence, dating by lichenometry in the former area may span around 5,000 years, whereas in the latter it could be under 1,000 years (Porter 1981). Among the oldest lichens so far reported is one in the Colorado Front Range whose age is about 6,000 years (Benedict 1967) and another in Swedish Lapland which might be a staggering 9,000 years old (Denton and Karlén 1973).

   Added to the already mentioned regional contrasts in lichen survival times, are variations in growth rates due to micro-environmental influences. In arctic regions, for example, such influences would include rock type, exposure to abrasion, shading, temperature, moisture, stability of substrate, and length of growing season. For dating by lichenometry to be successful, the effects of these influences must be known and techniques for establishing growth rates have to be accurate. Such techniques can adopt either a direct or indirect approach. The first involves measuring the growth of lichen thalli over a long period and is therefore not very practical. More realistic and worth while is the indirect method which seeks to ascertain the diameters of the largest lichens occurring on surfaces of known age (e.g. walls), it being assumed that these represent the oldest specimens. Observa-

Table 2.2   Some recorded growth rates of crustose lichen species

SPECIES	AVERAGE ANNUAL INCREASE IN MM (Radial growth)
Lecanora muralis	3.8
Diploschistes scruposus	2.2
Lecidea coarctata	1.4
Rhizocarpon geographicum	1.0
Rinodina oreina	0.6

Source: Richardson 1975.

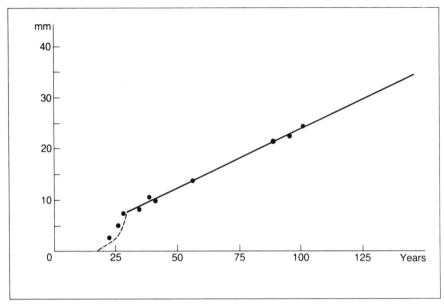

Fig 2.2   The growth of *Rhizocarpon geographicum* in the Valfurva. (After Belloni, 1970).

tions indicate that many crustose lichens develop very slowly at first. Then follows a period of accelerated growth until finally a slow, but constant rate of development is established (Fig. 2.2) (Benedict 1967: Andrews and Webber 1969).

When the largest examples of a particular species have been measured at numerous sites, a map showing lines of equal growth (*isophyses*) can be constructed, thereby providing further evidence of the progress of glacier retreat (Andrews and Webber 1969; Richardson 1975).

3. The most valuable lichen for determining glacier fluctuations is *Rhizocarpon geographicum* which has been used in places as far apart as the Colorado Front Range (Benedict 1967), the Alps (Belloni 1970, 1973) and New Zealand (Burrows and Orwin 1971). Innes (1981), however, points out that the taxonomy of this species has yet to be properly elucidated and that many people use the term *R. geographicum* for the whole *Geographicum* group. Of other lichens which have been applied to the study of glacier variations, *R. alpicola* has the merit of being widespread and long-lived in Scandinavia, though it is virtually confined to that area (Denton and Karlén 1973), while *Alectoria minuscula* has proved valuable in studies on Baffin Island (Andrews and Webber 1969).

Trees are another vegetational grouping which has been used to determine glacier fluctuations. Thus, Godwin-Austen found trees in the Karakoram which had been killed due to flooding by an ice-dammed lake at a time of glacier expansion. Having noted the area covered by dead trees, he was able to calculate the dimensions of the former lake (Godwin-Austen 1864). Similar observations have been made in the Lago Argentino district of Patagonia where hundreds of trees were killed either by flooding due to the formation of ice-dammed lakes or by the advancing Moreno glacier (Nichols and Miller 1952). It should not, however, be imagined that trees which have succumbed to an advancing glacier were necessarily killed by its bulldozing effect. Several alternative causes of death have been established by Grant and Higgins (1913) during work in the Prince William Sound and Kenai peninsula areas of Alaska. In 1909 they found trees which were being attacked not only by advancing ice, but also by meltwater streams and by waves generated when terminal sections of the Columbia glacier fell into the adjacent bay. They likewise observed trees which had been killed when they were partly submerged by outwash from the Bainbridge and Yalik glaciers. Although such examples complicate attempts to define precisely former ice limits, Grant and Higgins nevertheless felt that in the general absence of contemporary observations, these limits can often be reasonably well located by examining trees and their remains. This view has been supported by Cooper (1937) who worked in the Glacier Bay region of Alaska.

Cooper, in fact, described examples of the classic situation whereby a forest succumbed to an advancing glacier, but then had its tree stumps re-exposed during a later period of ice retreat. In the Alps, where evidence of such events has frequently been reported over the last 200 years, the value of trees for determining glacier fluctuations has been extended by C_{14} dating and growth-ring analysis. Unfortunately, the application of these techniques is not without problems, as Röthlisberger *et al.* (1980) have shown with regard to C_{14} dating. These problems are compounded by the need to establish an unequivocal link between the C_{14} age of a wood specimen and glacier fluctuations. Where tree remnants are clearly *in situ*, as is often the case on the valley floor downstream from the present glacier terminus, such a link would appear to be established. Problems arise, however, with the so-called 'avalanche wood', for this will have been transported to the area in front of the glacier by various types of slope movement or by storms before being overridden by ice. The C_{14} date of such material is therefore a less reliable indicator of glacier fluctuations. Despite these problems, C_{14} dating is indisputably advancing our knowledge of glacier behaviour. In particular it is enabling the pattern and timing of glacier fluctuations to be determined over several thousand years and it is helping to show that moraines in widely scattered localities were built up over a long period (Schneebeli 1976; Röthlisberger 1976; Roethlisberger and Schneebeli 1979; Röthlisberger *et al.* 1980). Glacial history can also be elucidated using tree rings, for these may have a direct or indirect relationship to variations in ice cover. An example of a *direct* relationship would occur when an advancing glacier disturbs and tilts a tree, but does not kill it (this happened, for instance, in 1909 during a thrust of the Columbia glacier) (Grant and Higgins 1913). Because of such interference, the tree may develop asymmetrical growth rings (Lawrence 1950). *Indirect* relationships between tree-ring characteristics and glacier fluctuations stem from the fact that both are influenced by similar things (e.g. summer temperatures). Thus, Lamarche and Fritts (1971) showed that ring widths of *Pinus cembra* near the upper tree-line at Riederalp (Switzerland) and Patscherkofel (Austria) displayed a strong negative correlation with the percentage of advancing glaciers in the two countries. As some *P. cembra* in the Alps are over 1,000 years old, this technique can assist our understanding of events during periods for which there is little documentary evidence. Studies in upper Gudbrandsdalen (Norway) have likewise demonstrated a good correlation between growth variations of *P. sylvestris* and fluctuations of Storbreen. Though the period covered was in this case only 250 years, the technique nevertheless provided information on glacier variations which could not have been acquired from other sources. There are, however, limitations to such an approach, mainly because trees and glaciers do not react in an identical way to summer temperatures and other environmental influences (Matthews 1977). Work on indirect relationships between tree rings and glacier fluctuations in the Alps has recently involved the use of X-ray dendroclimatology. The

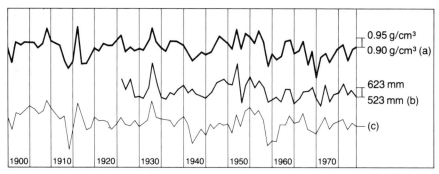

Fig 2.3 Maximum density of latewood (a and c) and glacier discharge (b) in Valais. (After Röthlisberger *et al*, 1980).

technique distinguishes between *earlywood* (the light part of a tree ring) and *latewood* (a ring's dark area). It entails X-raying the rings and scanning the density of their woods with a microdensitometer. Research indicates that latewood density in conifers on tree-lines throughout the Alps reflects the average temperature for July, August and September. It has also been found that tree-ring density curves correlate with glacier variations (Fig. 2.3) (Röthlisberger 1976; Röthlisberger *et al.* 1980).

Knowledge of glacier fluctuations during historic times has also been improved by the study of pollen, peat deposits and plant communities in areas close to present-day ice (e.g. Stork 1963; Ladurie 1967, 1972; Mayr 1968; Messerli *et al.* 1975). As with lichenometry and tree-ring analysis, these techniques should be used in conjunction with other methods, rather than separately. In this way, problems due to their individual shortcomings can be minimized.

Field measurements and historical documents

The best way to monitor glacier fluctuations is to observe them as they happen and to measure precisely the changes which occur. As far as the present book is concerned, interest lies not so much with measurements of the kind described by Paterson (1981) (i.e. determination of velocity and strain rate on the ice surface and at depth, etc.), but more with the precise recording of changes in the positions of glacier snouts. These changes are important because it is they above all which bring glaciers into contact with areas of human activity. Fortunately for present purposes, their measurement in the field has often been taken more intensively than has the monitoring of other forms of glacier change. To a lesser extent, however, fluctuations in the volume of ice (a topic which Paterson does examine) are also of interest in the present context because they too may have a bearing on human activity (e.g. glacier thickening may cause valley-side roads to be overrun).

Early work on the field measurement of glacier variations owes much to the scientist, F-A. Forel. In 1880–81 he began a network of observations in Switzerland which has operated continuously until the present and which now regularly monitors the snout position of more than 100 glaciers. After 1882 these measurements were recorded in *l'Annuaire du Club alpin suisse*, a publication which in 1925 changed to its present name *Les Alpes* (*Die Alpen*). Similar measurements have been carried out since 1897 in Germany and Austria (Kasser and Aellen 1976; Bachmann 1979; Vivian 1979). Hence, the Alpine countries possess the best records of glacier fluctuations determined by field measurement. Nevertheless, these records cover a woefully short period, even for the study of historic glacier variations, and are decidedly inadequate for work which encompasses longer time spans. In recent decades, the number of glaciers world-wide whose fluctuations are being methodically recorded has increased, as publications by Kasser (1967, 1973) and Müller (1977) show. However, this still leaves many glaciers whose variations are not being regularly and precisely observed.

If the field measurement of glacier variations is to achieve maximum value, universally accepted guidelines must be followed. They should include:

1. Annual measurements of the position of glacier termini should be made at the same time of year, so that the data obtained are genuinely comparable. Autumn is usually selected as the best period for such work, because it marks the end of the glacier mass balance year. Thus, Swiss observers are instructed to carry out measurements between 15 September and 15 October, though it is recognized that under certain circumstances these dates may have to be adjusted (Kasser 1967).

2. Measuring changes in the position of glacier termini should not only employ standardized and therefore comparable techniques, it must also be accurate in terms of the methods used and the care with which these are put into practice. As yet, standardization and accuracy of measurement have not been universally established (Müller 1977). None the less, bodies which collect data on glacier fluctuations may issue regulations in an effort to standardize their findings. This has happened, for example, with the Swiss Glacier Commission whose instructions to its observers have been reproduced by Kasser (1967).

3. Glacier fluctuations should be recorded in a standardized and preferably quantitative way, so that results from different localities may be easily compared. To this end, Müller (1977) has examined both the advantages and the difficulties of computerizing such data.

Glacier mapping can also produce valuable information about fluctuations in the extent and thickness of ice cover, especially when it is repeated at uniform intervals, thereby enabling changes to be regularly monitored. Although glaciers are mapped by field survey, the products of mapping inevitably become historical documents. A good example of this is Forbes's early map of the Chamonix glaciers which has appeared in various editions of his classic book on the western Alps (e.g. Forbes 1855, 1900). Good, modern glacier maps are contained in publications by Kasser (1967, 1973) and Müller (1977), and there is a discussion of the problems of glacier mapping in the *Canadian Journal of Earth Sciences* (vol. 3, no. 6, 1966). As with the measurement of changes in glacier length and thickness, mapping demands adherence to guidelines and a degree of standardization and quantification, especially if results from different localities are to be successfully compared (Kick 1966). In part, standardization can be achieved by workers following agreed instructions, such as those which have been issued by *Norges Geografiske Oppmåling* and were discussed by Hoel and Werenskiold (1962).

From its earliest days photography has been used to record the state of glaciers. Thus, in 1850 daguerreotypes were made of the lake which formed due to expansion of the Gurgler glacier (Ötztal Alps). Also significant was the introduction of photogrammetry by S. Finsterwalder who used it first to survey the Vernagt glacier in 1888–89. During the years which followed, other photogrammetric work was undertaken in the Ötztal Alps (e.g. by Blümcke and Hess who surveyed the Hochjoch glacier in 1893) (Rudolph 1963). Until 1923 surveys had to be carried out using ground photogrammetry, a technique which fortunately works well in glaciated high mountains because suitable viewpoints are usually available. Since then aerial photogrammetry has been developed and widely applied to glacier mapping. The techniques of photogrammetry and their value to glacier studies have been discussed by R. Finsterwalder (1954) and Konecny (1966).

Another fruitful line of inquiry has been to compare the modern appearance of glaciers with views of them by early photographers and pre-twentieth-century artists. The merits of this approach have been clearly demonstrated by Ladurie (1967, 1972) and Messerli et al. (1975, 1978). These latter in particular have done remarkable work by uncovering 486 pre-twentieth-century views of the two Grindelwald glaciers. They do, however, admit that the approach is complicated by problems. For example, the accurate dating of an engraving may be impossible because reproductions often appeared well after the initial drawing was made. Furthermore, engravers were not necessarily averse to changing details of the artist's original, which raises the question of the accuracy to be expected from non-photographic means of landscape depiction. Some indication of this may be gained by comparing the present appearance of long-lasting geomorphological features (peaks, ridges, etc.) with how they are shown on early engravings and paintings. If these features appear closely similar in both instances, it is likely that the glacier has been drawn accurately in the early illustrations. Moreover, engravings and paintings of high artistic quality also tend to possess accuracy. Their value may, however, be reduced if they show a glacier from a viewpoint which is quite different from that of other illustrations. Despite these problems, non-photographic landscape illustrations have proved useful when researching glacier fluctuations over a period which extends back at least to the seventeenth century.

Written descriptions of glaciers may extend the record into even earlier periods. Thus, in 1546 Sebastian Münster gave a precise account of the Rhône glacier tongue (Ladurie 1967, 1972), while around 1590 Oddur Einarsson mentioned that Icelandic glaciers were becoming larger (Thorarinsson 1960). The usefulness of such descriptions to modern scholars clearly depends on their accuracy, together with the amount and precision of the details they contain. An article by Ingram, Underhill and Farmer (1981), though dealing with the study of climate in historic times, represents a valuable assessment of the problems in using documentary records and makes numerous comments which are pertinent to the investigation of glacier fluctuations during recent centuries.

Other data sources

In several places (e.g. the Alps, Caucasus, Himalayas) there are legends and songs which tell how the extent of glaciers was different in the past. Some writers have considered oral traditions of doubtful value in the study of glacier fluctuations, but work by F. Röthlisberger (1974) in the Col d'Hérens area (Valais) has demonstrated that this view is not necessarily accurate. In fact, the legends which he discussed all seem to be founded on truth and can therefore be used along with data from other sources to clarify the history of glacier fluctuations. Röthlisberger has also shown that archaeological and etymological investigations can contribute towards an understanding of glacier behaviour. Thus, identifying the lines of ancient routeways and analysing place-name origins were other techniques which proved helpful when defining former ice margins in the Col d'Hérens area.

PATTERNS OF GLACIER FLUCTUATIONS DURING HISTORIC TIMES

One of F. Röthlisberger's (1974) more interesting conclusions was that during the

Roman period glacier termini in the Zermatt region were no further forward than in 1920. Unfortunately, information of this kind is rare for the first 1,500 years of the Christian era, as also is evidence for the human impact of glacier variations. Our current understanding of this period must therefore rely on a broadly sketched picture of events, rather than on detailed and precise knowledge. The few specific facts which are available indicate that climate was relatively good and glaciers fairly small during the eleventh and twelfth centuries, but that between 1200 and 1550 there was a trend towards climatic deterioration and glacier expansion at widely scattered localities (e.g. the Alps, Scandinavia, North America) (Grove 1979; Porter 1981). This trend culminated in a protracted period of glacier enlargement which at many places began with a marked climatic decline in the second half of the sixteenth century and lasted until around 1860–70 (Fig. 2.4). In a few localities (e.g. the Karakoram: Mercer 1975b) it even persisted to the early twentieth century. Throughout the present book the well-known term *Little Ice Age* will be used for this period of glacier enlargement, though it is appreciated that alternatives (e.g. Fernau stage) exist and that the term itself is not entirely appropriate. Roethlisberger and Schneebeli (1979), for example, have described it as 'exaggerated' for the sound reason that glacier termini have equalled or surpassed their Little Ice Age positions on a number of occasions during the Holocene. Yet, despite these problems of terminology, there can be no doubting the importance of the Little Ice Age as an environmental event and as an influence on human activity. Glacier expansion was a world-wide phenomenon at this time, although ice margins did not necessarily oscillate in a closely synchronized fashion, a point demonstrated by comparing the patterns of glacier fluctuations in the Alps with those in Scandinavia. Even within a single mountain range (e.g. the Mont Blanc massif: Grove 1966), the fluctuations of individual glaciers were not always synchronous. On the other hand, Porter (1981) has warned that the apparent lack of synchronization may in some cases result from the inaccuracy of dating techniques. The problem clearly needs further investigation.

After the Little Ice Age there was a world-wide contraction of glaciers. In many localities this became so pronounced that a number of ice masses disappeared altogether. For example, during one fifty-year period no less than thirty-two glaciers vanished from the Italian slopes of the western Alps (Vivian 1979). Such a trend has meant that between 1877 and 1932 the glacierized area of Switzerland contracted by 25 per cent (Mercanton 1954), while from 1882 to 1965 that of the Caucasus shrank by 27 per cent (Kotliakov and Touchinski 1974). Yet, shrinkage of ice-covered areas does not necessarily lead to a diminution in the number of glaciers: on the contrary, it sometimes increases their total. Hence, in 1890 there were 1,412 glaciers in the Caucasus, whereas by the 1960s their number stood at 2040, owing to fragmentation of the larger ice masses (Kotliakov and Touchinski 1974). At many places glacier termini have retreated by between 1 km and 3 km in the last 120 or so years, though local factors have produced variations outside these limits. In some cases, termini have retreated only a few hundred metres during this period (e.g. that of the Giétro glacier in Valais which is at a high altitude: Roethlisberger and Schneebeli 1979). By contrast, exceptional amounts of retreat have also been recorded. A striking example was the loss of 14.5 km of ice at Glacier Bay (Alaska) between 1907 and 1940 (Miller 1963). Equally, other glaciers have fluctuated just as decisively *against* the world-wide trend. For instance, the Brenva glacier on the Italian side of the Mont Blanc range advanced strongly between about 1914 and 1940. Though in the first seven years of this period other glacier termini were also moving forward, after that the Brenva became exceptional as it advanced 400–500 m over the next twenty years, perhaps

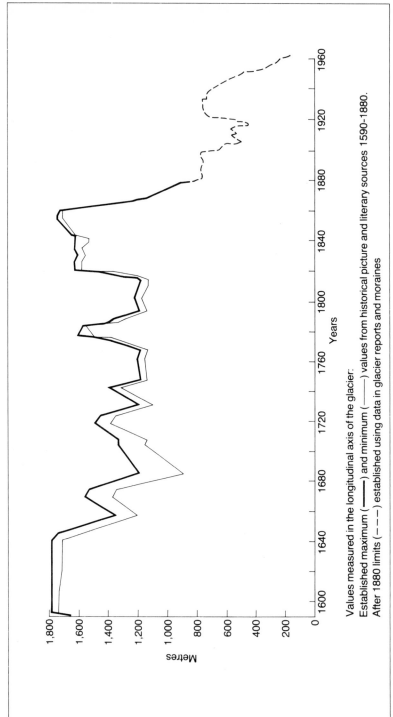

Values measured in the longitudinal axis of the glacier:
Established maximum (——) and minimum (——) values from historical picture and literary sources 1590–1880.
After 1880 limits (– – –) established using data in glacier reports and moraines

Fig 2.4   Snout variations of the Lower Grindelwald glacier 1590–1970. (After Messerli *et al*, 1975, 1978).

due to the effects of a landslide which fell on to the ice in 1920 (Mercer 1975a; Bachman 1979). Similarly, around the turn of the century a number of Karakoram glaciers (e.g. the Hasanabad, Mutshual and Yengutz) underwent striking amounts of expansion (Hayden 1907; Mercer 1975b).However, those advances which occurred between 1860 and 1960 have rarely constituted anything even vaguely like a wide-spread trend towards glacier enlargement. The nearest approaches to this were, for example, during the minor thrusts of the 1890s and around 1920 in the Alps, and during the 1940s and 1950s in the the Cascade Mountains of North America (Field 1975a; Röthlisberger *et al.* 1980).

Indeed, the 1950s, and more especially the 1960s, ushered in the most pronounced and widespread glacier advances for 100 years. Recent decades have also witnessed the greatest decline in temperatures for at least 200 years (Lamb 1977). Yet, there is no certainty that these events will be followed by a marked and enduring trend towards world-wide glacier expansion. Predicting long-term glacier variations is not within the ability of present-day scientists, which makes it all the more difficult to respond satisfactorily to the hazards they might cause.

CHAPTER 3
GLACIER FLUCTUATIONS AND SETTLEMENT

Particularly during the Little Ice Age, individual buildings and even whole villages were abandoned or seriously threatened because of expanding glaciers, meltwater streams and deteriorating climate. Unfortunately, very few people have taken the trouble to investigate these hazards, so their importance has not been properly evaluated. Moreover, the sketchiness of available data has led to conflicting remarks being made on the subject. For example, Bachmann (1979) claims that Alpine homes have rarely been damaged by glaciers, whereas Vivian (1979) says that many of the region's hamlets were destroyed during the advances of the seventeenth century. Given that details of encounters between glaciers and settlements were often written in vague language or simply went unrecorded, it is impossible to uncover the full story of what happened. Yet, our understanding of the problem could be improved by drawing together relevant information from throughout the published literature. This the present chapter attempts to do under three headings: distribution, timing, and nature of the hazard.

DISTRIBUTION OF THE HAZARD

The Alps

The impact of glacier expansion on settlements has been particularly marked in the Chamonix valley. Hence, a knowledge of events in this area will always be invaluable for anyone wishing to understand the problem of glacier fluctuations in its wider context. As these events have been fairly well documented and researched, it has been possible to compile the detailed summary which forms Table 3.1. This shows that four villages (Bonnenuict, La Bonneville, Le Châtelard and Les Rosières) were totally destroyed by advancing glaciers and meltwater torrents during the first half of the seventeenth century: none of these has been rebuilt, though the name Les Rosières is still found on maps, occurring between Les Praz and Chamonix. Other villages, such as La Rosière (near Argentière) and Le Fouilly, experienced severe glacier damage, but managed to survive, while Les Bois was abandoned around 1600 due to the proximity of the Mer de Glace, though it was later reoccupied and still exists today. In addition, the settlements of Le Tour, Argentière. Les Tines, Les Praz, Les Bossons and Montquart were all at various times closely approached by their local glaciers, but were not overrun nor damaged too severely (Fig. 3.1).

Table 3.1 Glacier hazards and settlements in the Chamonix valley (This table includes all types of glacier hazards which have affected settlement in the Arve valley upstream from Les Houches. It has been compiled from the following sources: Viollet-le-Duc 1877; Collingwood 1884; Blanchard 1913; Rabot 1920; Sourbier 1950; Glaister 1951; Grove 1966; Ladurie 1967, 1972; Vincent 1976; Vivian 1976, 1979; Bachmann 1979.)

DATES	EVENTS
About 1600	Advancing glaciers destroy 7 houses in the Argentière–La Rosière area, 2 at La Bonneville, 12 at Le Châtelard, and the entire hamlet of Bonnenuict. The Mer de Glace came so close to Les Bois that the village was damaged and had to be abandoned. It was also near Les Tines
1610	Water from the Argentière glacier destroys 8 houses and 5 barns. Torrents from the Bossons glacier severely damage Le Fouilly. 3 houses, 7 barns, and 1 mill destroyed at La Bonneville. Mer de Glace still close to Les Bois and causing damage
1613 or 1614	Glacial meltwater completes the destruction of La Bonneville
1616	Argentière glacier adjoining La Rosière. About 6 houses remaining at Le Châtelard, though only 2 inhabited. Glacier very close. At some time between 1642 and 1700 the village was finally abandoned and has never been rebuilt. Its inhabitants are thought to have settled at Les Tines
1628–30	Falls of snow and glaciers in the Chamonix valley. Flooding of the Arve due to glacial meltwater
1640s	Glaciers came close to Le Tour, Argentière, La Rosière, Les Tines, Les Bois, Les Praz and Les Bossons. 1641: Les Rosières (*not* La Rosière, but a village near Chamonix) destroyed by a flood from the Mer de Glace. 1642: avalanche of snow and ice destroyed 2 homes at Le Tour, and killed 4 cows and 8 sheep. 1641–43: property flooded and ruined by torrents from the Bossons glacier
1714	Several villages still threatened by glaciers
About 1730	Mer de Glace less than 400 m from the nearest houses at Les Bois
1818–20	Glaciers again almost at Le Tour, Montquart and Les Bois (the Mer de Glace was only 20 m from this last village). The Argentière glacier was little more than 300 m from the old centre of Argentière village
1826	Mer de Glace showering debris on to the chalets below
1835	*Séracs* from the Mer de Glace threaten to fall on Les Bois
1850	Mer de Glace about 50 m from Les Bois and causing blocks of ice to fall towards Les Tines
1852	Several glacier avalanches in the Chamonix valley due to warm winds and heavy rains
1878	*Débâcle* from the Mer de Glace. Houses evacuated as a safety measure; fields flooded. Similar outbursts had occurred in 1610 and 1716
1920	*Débâcle* from the Mer de Glace floods the cellars and ground floors of many buildings in Chamonix. Much land inundated*

Table 3.1   (cont'd)

DATES	EVENTS
1949	Avalanche from the Glacier du Tour kills 6 people. The worst ice avalanche in the French Alps since the Glacier de Tête Rousse disaster of 1892 (Ch. 5)†
1977	Le Tour threatened by glacier avalanche

* Bachmann (1979) gives the date of this event as 1912, but Sourbier (1950) and Vivian (1976) say it occurred in 1920.

† Several authors (e.g. Grove 1966; Bachmann 1979; Vivian 1979) describe only one such event, that of 14 August 1949. Vincent (1976) also mentions a single event, but attributes it to an ice avalanche in 1957 which killed 7 people.

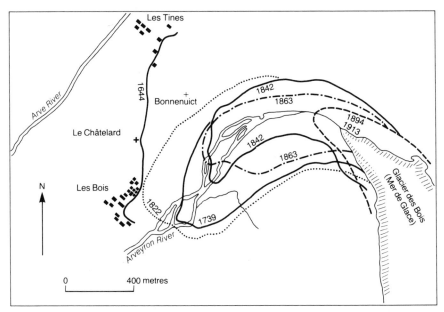

Fig 3.1   Settlements and variations of the Mer de Glace (1644 to 1919) (After Rabot, 1920)

The Chamonix archives indicate that during the early years of the seventeenth century people elsewhere in Savoy also suffered glacier damage. Although the places in question were named (Samoëns, Sis, Vallon, Montpitton and Morillon), no information was apparently given regarding the nature of this damage (Ladurie 1967, 1972). It is therefore impossible to tell if buildings were among the things affected. By contrast, no such doubts exist about the impact of early seventeenth-century advances by the Grindelwald glaciers. Around 1600 the upper glacier overran two houses and five barns, while the nearby lower glacier caused four houses to be evacuated. An engraving of 1640 shows houses near the lower glacier and mentions in its caption that these had to be moved because of the advancing ice (Richter 1891; Ladurie 1967, 1972). In 1673–4, an article published by the Royal Society also contained an illustration of the Lower Grindelwald area, probably based on the 1640 engraving. The buildings shown on this illustration were, we are told, a long way from the glacier when erected, but became threatened by ice during a subsequent advance (Anon, 1673–4; Coolidge 1908). Several kilometres to the east of the Grindelwald area is the Gauli glacier which has also been responsible for destroying buildings. Evidence of this appeared in 1829 when the remains of a chalet were ejected from the snout of the glacier. These probably came from one of the buildings connected with an area of former pastureland known as the *Blümlisalp* (Bachmann 1979). South of the Grindelward–Gauli area, in the canton of Valais, there are further localities where glacier advances have threatened or destroyed buildings (see Ch 6).

In the Italian Alps glacier fluctuations have caused problems for buildings in the Val Veni and Val Ferret. An early advance of the Brenva glacier into the Val Veni was apparently responsible for overrunning the site of St Jean de Pertuis, though the village had already been destroyed and its inhabitants killed by a previous catastrophe. According to Vivian (1979), who was quoting a parchment dating from 1300, the catastrophe was due to an *éboulement de la montagne*. This is presumably a reference to some sort of landslide, not unlike the one which collapsed on to the Brenva glacier in 1920. On the other hand, the oral version of the story which was given to Forbes tells how the Brenva glacier used to overhang St Jean, until one day it avalanched on to the village with disastrous results. The testimony of a child, that he heard the chanting of vespers and saw a procession which emerged from the ice and then returned to it, must no doubt have supported the belief that the remains of the village were still lying under the glacier (Forbes 1900). Near the site of St Jean de Pertuis, but on higher ground, is the chapel of Notre Dame de la Guérison: this too has had some interesting encounters with the Brenva glacier. For example, in 1818–19, during a time of glacier expansion, the ice was pressing so hard against the rocks on which the chapel stood that they fractured. The foundations of the building were thereby damaged and the whole structure had to be pulled down in 1820. A new chapel was erected in a safer position the following year and was in no danger for the next two decades because of glacier retreat. Then, a new advance began and by 1850 the ice surface had risen almost to the level of the chapel floor. However, in that year the Brenva started a long period of contraction which has ensured that the chapel has had no subsequent interference from glaciers. Nearby, the village of Entrèves has also on occasion been threatened by an advancing Brenva glacier. Thus, in about 1780 and again between 1810 and 1820 the distance between the two was only 1000 m or perhaps less. Similarly, the neighbouring Val Ferret has experienced glacier hazards. For instance, during the early part of the Little Ice Age an advancing Triolet glacier overran the houses and meadows of Ameiron (Forbes 1900; Grove 1966).

In the eastern Alps there seem to have been fewer examples of glaciers threatening or destroying buildings. Among the most noteworthy is the case of Ganda (Gampen), a hamlet in the Ortler Massif which was evacuated in 1818–19 due to the close approach of the Solda glacier. This became hazardous because it underwent a pronounced surge and increased its length by over 1200 m during 1817–18. Later, in the middle of the nineteenth century, villages in the Ötztal Alps were threatened by glaciers. For example, the Mittelbergferner came to within 800 m of Mittelberg, whose inhabitants understandably offered regular prayers for deliverance from the advancing ice (Rudolph 1963; Bachmann 1979).

Iceland

According to Denton (1975b), many Icelandic glaciers have destroyed agricultural land and buildings. It is difficult, however, to evaluate the precise impact of this hazard because contemporary reports have often been inexact. The evidence, nevertheless, suggests that most of the buildings affected by expanding glaciers were from two main areas. One of these lies along the southern edges of the Vatnajökull ice-cap, while the other is on the Westfjord peninsula, around the margins of the Drangajökull.

In recent centuries, no Icelandic glacier advanced more strongly than did Breidamerkurjökull, a southern outlet of Vatnajökull. It consequently overran a number of farm buildings. The trouble seems first to have arisen in the late seventeenth century, for it is known that by 1700 farms had already suffered due to glacier harassment. One of these, Breidármörk, was deserted in 1698: by 1712 the buildings were in ruins and were close to being overrun by the glacier. A little to the west, the Fjall farm was having similar troubles. Its abandonment probably occurred before 1694, though it was not until the early years of the eighteenth century that its ruins eventually disappeared beneath the advancing Hrútárjökull. After more than two centuries of being covered by ice, the Breidármörk and Fjall farms have now been re-exposed due to glacier retreat (Fig. 3.2). The Svinafell farm, which lies to the west of the Breidármörk – Fjall area, has had an equally interesting, though somewhat different history. It too was established at an early period of Icelandic colonization. However, throughout its long existence the glacier threat has never been far away. Thus, in 1794 the Svinafellsjökull was close to the farm and as recently as 1865 it was within five minutes walking distance. The former proximity of the glacier can be

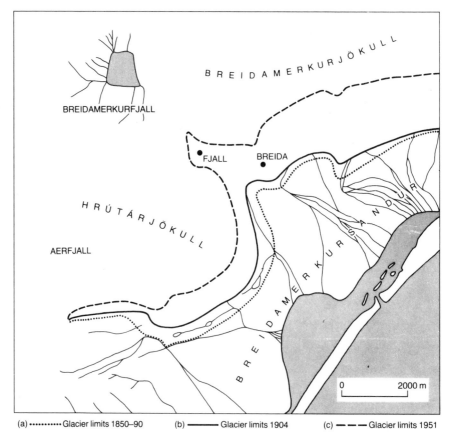

(a) ··········· Glacier limits 1850–90   (b) ———— Glacier limits 1904   (c) — — — Glacier limits 1951

Fig 3.2   Glacier limits and farms in the Breidamerkurfjall area of southern Iceland. (After Thorarinsson, 1956).

appreciated even today because of the large moraines which are only a few hundred metres from the farm buildings. A not dissimilar story can be told for the Heinaberg farm, which lay well to the east of the other areas mentioned. In about the mid eighteenth century the Heinabergsjökull was threatening this farm, though there was apparently no break in habitation at that time. More recently, during the nineteenth century, glacier advances have again destroyed farms, this time in the south-eastern Breidamerkurjökull area (Thorarinsson 1943, 1956, 1958).

A second area where glaciers have harassed settlements occurs around the edges of Drangajökull, in the valleys of Kaldalón, Leirufjördur, Reykjafjördur and Tharalátursfjördur. Two farms called Lónhóll and Trimbilstadir, were supposedly destroyed by the glacier in the Kaldalón valley, though available information does not say exactly what happened. John and Sugden (1962) mention a local belief that Trimbilstadir was destroyed by ice around 1600, whereas Eythorsson (1935) merely reports that farm ruins which were visible in 1931 could not be seen in 1710 (?due to being covered by ice). Both articles also quote the remark published in 1780 by O. Olavius that Lónhóll was overwhelmed by a glacier *débâcle* in 1741, but John and Sugden, for reasons not given, are unwilling to accept that Lónhóll and Trimbilstadir were in fact destroyed. They suggest instead that during the first half of the eighteenth century Kaldalónsjökull was so close and its meltwater so troublesome that agriculture must have been impossible. It would therefore have been necessary to abandon the farms. On the other hand, they admit that it is equally likely the farms were deserted before this time.

Another outlet of Drangajökull is said to have destroyed farms in the valley of Leirufjördur. One of these, Öldugil, probably became untenanted in the fifteenth century owing to glacier *débâcles*. In 1710 the ruins of the farm were close to the glacier and its land was beneath the ice. Similarly, farms were harassed by the glacier in Reykjafjördur, though once again the reports are irritatingly vague. However, one which dates from 1710 does mention an untenanted farm, Knittilstadir, as being close to the glacier at that time. More recently, Eythorsson has quoted a local tradition that this farm used to lie beneath the ice. Other reports claim that the glacier in Tharalátursfjördur has destroyed inhabited land, particularly due to outbursts of mud and water. Magnússon, writing in 1710, says that these events did not occur within living memory (Eythorsson 1935).

Norway

The worst areas for glacier damage have been the outlet valleys of Jostedalsbreen, between Sognefjord and Nordfjord. Thus, around 1693 a glacier and its meltwater in Kjenndalen destroyed six barns. Again, during 1728 the occupants of Tungøyane farm in Oldendalen, on the north-west edges of Jostedalsbreen, abandoned their homes for a new location which they thought was better protected from the advancing Åbrekkebreen. Unfortunately, in 1743 these new homes were suddenly overwhelmed by falling ice and rock and only two people survived. The nearby Åbrekke farm was also extensively damaged. Several months previously Nigardsbreen, an outlet glacier on the eastern side of Jostedalsbreen, had likewise destroyed a farm (Hoel and Werenskiold 1962; Grove and Battagel 1981).

A second area where glacier advances have destroyed farm buildings and agricultural land is around the edges of the Svartisen ice-caps. For example, in the 1720s Engabreen in Holandsfjord overran the farm at Storstenøren and badly damaged its neighbour, Fonnøren (Hoel and Werenskiold 1962; Theakstone 1965; Worsley and Alexander 1976).

Caucasus

The Caucasus, like the Alps, have witnessed a close interplay between glaciers and man. Observations made in the northern valleys of the central Caucasus around 1900 mention old ruins existing near the margins of glaciers. They are presumably indicative of a time when the climate was milder and the glaciers smaller than at present, thus enabling settlement to penetrate deeply into these mountain valleys. Evidence that glacier advances helped to destroy settlements may be found in the region's songs and legends. For example, one of the songs tells how a glacier (probably Lednik Khalde) advanced more than 6 km and partly destroyed the village of Ushkul (Horvath and Field 1975).

Karakoram

On occasion, the Chogo Lungma glacier has interfered with agriculture and settlement in the Basha valley. Early in the nineteenth century the distance between this glacier and the village of Arandu was 2.5 km, but by 1861 only 365 m separated the two. Arandu was established in the twelfth or thirteenth centuries, so the glacier's 1861 position cannot have been exceeded for at least several hundred years. In a more recent example, from around the turn of the present century, the Yengutz glacier very rapidly advanced a distance of about 3 km and consequently overran a number of mills and cultivated fields. A little later, in 1913, the snout of the Pasu glacier was only a short distance from a village of the same name (Fig. 3.3), while in 1933 a glacier was very close to Bad Swat. Its inhabitants believed that the ice regularly advanced almost to the village, which they therefore prepared to evacuate, but then it just as regularly retreated (Godwin-Austen 1864; Hayden 1907; Mason 1914, 1935; Schomberg 1934; Mercer 1975b).

Alaska

Miller (1963), in a regional survey of Alaskan glacier fluctuations, describes two examples of where advancing ice has come into contact with villages. One of these

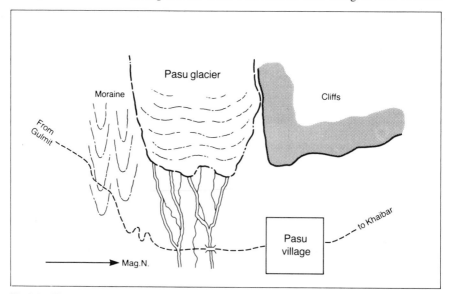

Fig 3.3 The village and glacier of Pasu (Karakoram), August 1913. (After Mason, 1914).

occurred some time after 1794, for in that year Captain Vancouver saw a deserted Indian village close to the terminus of the Brady glacier (Lituya Bay area). During the next 100 years this glacier advanced 9.6 km and covered the village with over 330 m of ice. Miller's second example is from the St Elias region and was given to him by an old Indian whose people had settled on the once green shores of Icy Bay. Unfortunately, there came a time (probably in the early or mid seventeenth century) when a very rapid advance of the Guyot glacier forced these people to leave their village.

TIMING OF THE HAZARD

From a twentieth-century viewpoint it might appear that medieval settlers in the Alps, Iceland and elsewhere were remarkably ignorant of the dangers which glaciers can pose, for they not infrequently built their homes and began farming in areas which were subsequently overrun by the advances of the Little Ice Age. Yet, it must be remembered that at the time of colonization glaciers were probably small and posed no threat to these areas, nor did stories of earlier catastrophies exist. Where the date of colonization is known, it is usually apparent that the decision to settle was a reasonable one, as in most cases several centuries were to elapse before glaciers became really threatening. Thus, the Fjall farm on the southern margins of Vatnajökull was established in about 900, but it was not until around 1700 that it was abandoned prior to being overrun by the advancing Hrútárjökull (Ahlmann and Thorarinsson 1937). Anyone who is tempted to criticize the settlement policy of medieval farmers as it related to glaciers would do well to reflect on the consequences were a future advance to exceed by 2 or 3 km the known maxima of historic times.

Although the glacial hazards of the Little Ice Age originated with the beginnings of climatic deterioration in the thirteenth and fourteenth centuries, it was not until around 1600 that advancing ice started to damage and destroy buildings near places such as Chamonix and Grindelwald. The high point in glacier expansion which caused these misfortunes lasted for about fifty years. In the Chamonix valley it has been possible to identify within this period three decades when glaciers were especially troublesome – 1600–20 and the 1640s (Table 3.1). According to Eythorsson (1935), glaciers also reached a high point at around the same time in Iceland, though here as in Norway, the records of danger and destruction tend not to begin for nearly another 100 years (i.e. during the final decade of the seventeenth century) (Grove and Battagel 1981). There are, however, a few exceptions to this which would seem to indicate an earlier phase of settlement damage by advancing glaciers (as, for example, in the case of some outlets of Drangajökull). Unfortunately, the available details are not very enlightening so, from current evidence, one must conclude that the *chief* period of settlement destruction by Icelandic and Norwegian glaciers took place during the last decade of the seventeenth and the first sixty years of the eighteenth centuries. This conclusion is supported by the fact that in the majority of cases the termini of these glaciers were then at one of their most advanced historical positions (Thorarinsson 1943; Hoel and Werenskiold 1962). Some decades later Alpine glaciers began another major thrust. This lasted from about 1810 to 1860 and again settlements were threatened or destroyed (e.g. near Chamonix and Zermatt). At the same time, glaciers were harassing individual buildings and villages in other parts of the world (e.g. in Iceland, Alaska and the Karakoram Mountains). Fortunately, the hazard then disappeared from many areas owing to glacier retreat, though it has persisted into the twentieth century at a few localities (e.g. in parts of the Karakoram). This means that on numerous occasions during the last 400 years there have been places where glaciers were harassing or destroying settlements.

NATURE OF THE HAZARD

It is hard to find reliable eyewitness accounts which describe precisely and in detail how an individual building or a village has succumbed to an advancing glacier. Even so, there can be little doubt that the process usually involves more than the overrunning of a settlement by an expanding body of ice. Lyell (1881), for example, has pointed out that morainic debris may be pushed against buildings shortly before the ice actually reaches them. Other hazards are caused by glacial meltwater streams. Thus, Blanchard (1913) describes how the village of Les Bois in the Chamonix valley was threatened during the early seventeenth century 'tant par les eaux que par l'approche du glacier'. The fickleness of meltwater streams is highlighted by the events of June 1980 when the principal torrent issuing from the Ghulkin glacier suddenly changed course and badly affected the Karakoram Highway (Derbyshire and Miller 1981). Further problems arise when ice falls from a glacier on to nearby buildings. In addition to the classic situation whereby ice (often in large quantities) is displaced over a considerable length of slope before reaching a settlement (see Ch. 5), it is possible to have buildings threatened or destroyed by short-distance falls from an adjacent glacier. Several examples of the latter have occurred in the Chamonix valley (e.g. at Le Tour in 1642, Les Bois in 1835 and Les Tines in 1850: Table 3.1). The cold associated with a nearby glacier must also have created severe problems, especially for peasants who were heavily dependent on local produce and whose homes were poorly insulated. Not surprisingly, this type of glacial and climatic stress has on occasion led to depopulation (as, for example, in the Zermatt region: Ch. 7).

The difficulties of elucidating the physical processes which have harassed settlements during periods of glacier advance are often compounded by uncertainties over the status of the buildings in question. These uncertainties are partly due to observations which have failed to distinguish between houses where people lived and buildings which were merely used as hay barns, cattle sheds and the like. Such a distinction is important not only because of the differing status of these various types of building, but also because in many places hay barns and cattle sheds were some distance from their owners' homes. Other uncertainties arise where observers have used the word 'farm' imprecisely. This is the case, for example, with some of the Icelandic literature, and it usually leaves the reader with no means of deciding if the word refers either to farm buildings or to the land associated with them, or both. Equally, there are problems of interpretation when an observer has not made clear the function of a building at the time it became threatened by glacier advance. While some buildings were in use during the onset of glacier harassment, others had probably been abandoned at an earlier period. Both situations have apparently occurred, for example, in Iceland. Among the more important non-glacial causes of farm desertion in that country were the plague of 1402–5, which killed between one-third and one-half of the population, the smallpox epidemic of 1707, volcanic eruptions and general climatic severity (see, for example, Ogilvie 1981). Some of these deserted farms were perhaps later overrun by glacial advances. Because observers may not have indicated if buildings were in use when glacier harassment began, erroneous interpretations have at times been suggested. The point is illustrated by the case of the St Petronella chapel at Grindelwald. Local tradition and the published literature have often maintained that this building was overrun by an advancing Lower Grindelwald glacier. However, the truth appears to be that the chapel was destroyed during the Reformation, and only later did the glacier expand to cover the site where it had been (de Beer 1950; Ladurie 1967, 1972).

Glacier expansion occurs more slowly and is less violent than ice avalanching and glacier flooding. Even when surging, glaciers give ample warning of increased danger and so pose virtually no threat to human life. Furthermore, there is usually time to dismantle a property which is at risk and salvage its contents. For several reasons, however, buildings were not always dismantled before being overrun by ice. People would, for instance, have been uncertain about glacier behaviour and might therefore have refused to move from their homes hoping that the ice would retreat before causing damage. In addition, the conservatism of peasants and their attachment to property may have hindered them from taking the best course of action in the circumstances. Hence, when they were finally obliged to leave there may have been time to salvage the contents of their home, though it was perhaps too late to dismantle the structure itself. On other occasions, buildings may simply have been left to the mercy of an advancing glacier, because they were not worth saving, as their associated land had already been covered by ice. Happily, some settlements abandoned in the face of an oncoming glacier did narrowly escape being overrun and were therefore recolonized when the danger abated. Owing to the difficulties of understanding glacier behaviour, expecially in prescientific times, one should not be over-critical of those peasants who made the wrong decisions. The problems they had in assessing glacier danger are to some degree illustrated by the history of the Svinafell farm in Iceland. As mentioned earlier, this farm has often been closely approached by the Svinafellsjökull throughout its long existence, yet the glacier has not had a decisive effect on its survival (Thorarinsson 1958). Today, the development of a more scientific approach is helping us to understand glacier behaviour and this in turn should increasingly permit a more satisfactory response to the problem. Unfortunately, the lessons of previous disasters are too often forgotten. Thus, many Alpine buildings were threatened or destroyed in the first half of the nineteenth century when glacier termini reached positions very similar to those of 200 years previously. Recent construction work in areas which were glacier covered at the Little Ice Age maxima is a clear indication that even in the modern scientific age we often fail to appreciate the true potential of glacier hazards.

There is then ample evidence to show that during recent centuries glacier expansion has created numerous problems for settlements. By contrast, only a few instances exist where it has proved at all beneficial. In one of these, the combined snout of the Stein and Steinlimmi glaciers (Switzerland) advanced to within 50 m of the Stein glacier hotel, whose guests were therefore provided with meat kept fresh by having been stored in the ice (Haefeli 1963) (Fig. 4.3, p. 40). This example illustrates in a modest way that glacier fluctuations can influence not only settlements, but also the economy of an area.

CHAPTER 4
ECONOMIC EFFECTS OF GLACIER FLUCTUATIONS

ICE FOR REFRIGERATION

Glaciers have been used for refrigeration purposes at a number of Alpine localities. This exploitation was obviously encouraged when settlements and glaciers were in close proximity, and before artificial refrigeration methods were invented. There are perhaps two main ways of using glaciers for refrigeration. One is to keep perishables stored within the ice, as they did for the meat which was served at the Stein glacier hotel. Likewise, a seventeenth-century report mentions that 'holes and caverns' in the Lower Grindelwald glacier were used to store game 'during the great heat, to make it keep sweet' (Anon 1673–4; Coolidge 1908). Glacier ice has also been quarried and transported, sometimes to quite distant localities. Again, the technique was long used at Grindelwald where it provided much employment. For example, in 1876 there were sixty workmen engaged in quarrying blocks of ice from the Lower Grindelwald glacier (Bachmann 1979). Since ice had an economic value, its exploitation sometimes gave rise to disputes and legal battles. Vivian (1979) mentions an example from Brides-les-Bains in the French Alps. The dispute, which arose in the mid nineteenth century, was between a family called Etiévant and the hoteliers of Brides. The main cause of the problem was not who should exploit the ice, but whether the hoteliers should be allowed to cross and thus damage the Etiévants' land on their way to and from the glacier. On both occasions when the case was heard, judgement was in favour of the Etiévants. Using Alpine glaciers for refrigeration purposes has nearly always involved the exploitation of their snout areas. An exception is, however, provided by the Theodul glaciers on the Swiss–Italian border. For many years, the Theodul pass at the head of these glaciers was a routeway for movement and commerce between the two countries. It was therefore convenient to leave perishables in the ice on the pass, so they would be fresh when collected by trading partners from over the watershed (Harriss 1970).

Glaciers have also been exploited for refrigeration purposes at localities outside the Alps. For example, in Norway ice used to be obtained mainly from three glaciers, Folgefonni, Strupbreen and Øksfjordjøkulen. The first of these was much exploited by the British and, as at Brides, workmen on one occasion fell foul of local farmers by trampling over and damaging their land. After the 1850s the Folgefonni trade declined when new storage techniques were introduced, making it easier to use lake ice. On the other hand, the collection of ice from Øksfjordjøkulen persisted until 1949. As this glacier once reached sea-level, blocks of ice could be gathered up after they had calved into the water. By 1937, however, this technique was no longer practicable because recession meant that the glacier had ceased to calve in the usual way.

It therefore became necessary to quarry the ice and transport it down to the sea via chutes. In 1949 this method also fell into disuse owing to the building of a refrigeration plant (Hoel and Werenskiold 1962; Reynolds 1979). Similarly, around the turn of the century, ice which became detached from the Shoup glacier (Alaska) was gathered for refrigeration purposes at Valdez and Fort Liscum (Grant and Higgins 1913).

WATER SUPPLY AND HYDROELECTRICITY

Man has found two principal uses for glacial meltwater. The longer-established and more important of these has been for drinking and irrigation: much newer, but rapidly expanding, is its use in the generation of hydroelectricity and for industrial purposes. Indeed, in some areas (e.g. the canton of Valais: Ch. 6) hydroelectric schemes and industry have now superseded irrigation systems as the chief users of glacial meltwater. All these forms of economic exploitation are, of course, heavily dependent on the amounts of meltwater available and therefore in turn on the fluctuations and 'health' of glaciers.

It has been estimated that the mountain glaciers and smaller ice-caps of the northern hemisphere are alone capable of supplying every person on Earth with 10 million gallons of fresh water (Field 1975a). Yet this figure is obviously much lower than the equivalent values for the maxima of the Little Ice Age. As early as the 1870s glacier shrinkage and its effect on water supplies was causing concern, and this led to the first systematic measurements of glacier variations (Matthes 1942). Since these were initiated, the glaciers of the western Alps, for example, have lost an amount of ice equivalent to twenty months of flood conditions on the Isère river at Grenoble (Vivian 1979). Not surprisingly, those glaciers which have become important as sources of water have often been studied intensively, so that their fluctuations are rather well known. An example is the Nisqually glacier in the United States whose importance is due to the fact that it supplies the Nisqually river upon which the city of Tacoma depends for hydroelectricity (Matthes 1942). The rivers of central Asia are also noted for the meltwater they contain, which some would say is as high as 30–40 per cent of total flow. For centuries these rivers have been crucial to the well-being of the areas through which they pass and efforts have long been made to keep river flow at the desired level. In part this has meant devising techniques for increasing glacier and snow ablation, an approach tried as early as the days of Alexander the Great. Usually, dark material is scattered on the ice/snow surface to hasten melting. For example, in 1959 aeroplanes spread coal dust on nineteen glaciers in the Tien Shan and during a single month helped increase meltwater production by 12.5 million m^3 (Freeberne 1965). The effectiveness of such techniques is, however, limited, not least by the finite nature of the glacier source material. Natural variations in the accumulation and melting of glacier ice therefore retain a paramount importance. It has indeed been claimed that were the glacier shrinkage of the last 120 years to continue for another few decades, the effects in some areas might be catastrophic. Because of the way they can influence water supplies, glacier fluctuations could even have an important effect on the world economy (Field 1975a).

Man's use of glacial meltwater for drinking and irrigation appears to have a long history in many areas, though it is often not known when it began. Doubtless there have been numerous instances of people simply extracting water from the local river, unaware that it was fed at least in part by a distant glacier. Other people, however, deliberately went in search of water and, finding that it appeared at the snout of a glacier, proceeded to guide it artificially to where it was needed. In this way systems of irrigation channels were developed, which were many kilometres in length and often traversed difficult terrain. There are few written records of these developments, though it can be assumed that in some, perhaps many areas they were encouraged by the climatic conditions and population demands of the medieval period. This was a time when glaciers were in a shrunken state, ablation was low and evaporation relatively high, so that any population pressure or attempts to expand cultivation would have caused people to look for additional water supplies. After constructing elaborate irrigation systems, people unfortunately found, especially in late medieval times, that glaciers were beginning to advance as climate deteriorated. Since the intakes of channels were often located close to glacier termini, expanding ice has from time to time overrun the higher parts of many irrigation networks. This happened, for example, due to advances by the Lys glacier on the Italian slopes of Monte Rosa (Bachmann 1979) and the Hasanabad glacier in the Karakoram (Mason 1935) (see also Ch. 6). Despite their prolonged retreat since the Little Ice Age, glaciers still constitute an important source of water for irrigation. This is particularly so in the Alay region where meltwater supports intensive agriculture and one of the highest population densities in the USSR (Horvath 1975). Glacier ablation is also important for agriculture in the Karakoram (Godwin-Austen 1864; Finsterwalder 1960; Mercer 1975b), the Himalayas (Mercer 1975b), the Hindu Kush (Mercer 1975c), China (Free-berne 1965; Lehr and Horvath 1975), and the Caucasus (Horvath and Field 1975).

Recently, there has been a growing interest in the possibility of transporting icebergs to arid regions where they could be used to augment freshwater supplies. Although the feasibility of this novel idea has yet to be demonstrated, much genuine scientific thought is being devoted to it. The world's reserves of fresh water are mainly contained within the glaciers of Antarctica, but significant amounts are also found in the Greenland ice sheet. Each year these huge glaciers spawn thousands of icebergs, though the rate at which they do so can vary. Thus, during the first half of the twentieth century the number of icebergs drifting into the Grand Banks/Ice Patrol area off Newfoundland remained steady. Then, in the 1950s and 1960s, the figure dropped sharply, while more recently there have been signs of a recovery. Despite such fluctuations, icebergs are always likely to be formed at an annual rate which is large enough for them to constitute an important source of fresh water. It has been estimated that, were it possible to utilize Antarctic icebergs, water could be provided for up to 60 million ha of agricultural land (Husseiny 1978; Reynolds 1979).

In a world which is increasingly turning towards the exploitation of renewable energy sources, glacial meltwater is becoming more and more attractive for the generation of power. Already, it is extensively used in large and complex schemes, such as the Grande Dixence in Switzerland (Bezinge 1966; Vivian 1979; Park 1980) (Chs. 6 and 8) and the Glockner-Kaprun in Austria (Mutton 1951; Péguy 1956), both of which supply appreciable percentages of their country's energy needs. The size of these undertakings ensures that they require huge amounts of water to operate at maximum capacity. Glacier fluctuations would obviously affect the supply of water to such power stations, as, for example, Tollner (1957) and Østrem (1972) have pointed out (Table 4.1). That this effect would always be significant, let alone disastrous is by no means a foregone conclusion. Rogstad, for instance, has maintained that the disappearance of Norwegian glaciers would have only a small impact on that country's hydroelectric power (HEP) production (Hoel and Werenskiold 1962). More research is needed, however, before an accurate evaluation of this matter is possible at all localities.

Table 4.1 Glacier mass balance and runoff (Nigardsbreen, western Norway) (After Østrem 1972).

(a) Decreased runoff due to positive glacier mass balance

YEAR	OBSERVED RUNOFF (10^6 m^3)	GLACIER MASS BALANCE (10^6 m^3)	THEORETICAL RUNOFF ('CORRECTED' TO ELIMINATE GLACIER INFLUENCE)
1964	166.9	+40.2	207.1
1965	154.2	+37.1	191.3

(b) Increased runoff due to negative glacier mass balance

YEAR	OBSERVED RUNOFF (10^6 m^3)	GLACIER MASS BALANCE (10^6 m^3)	THEORETICAL RUNOFF ('CORRECTED' TO ELIMINATE GLACIER INFLUENCE)
1969	249.3	−61.7	187.6
1970	210.9	−21.1	189.8

Further investigations are also required if the hydropower potential of a large ice body such as Greenland is to be fully utilized. Estimates not surprisingly indicate that this potential is considerable, for it almost equals the total 1974 consumption of electrical energy in Europe. Greenland has the advantage of possessing twelve to fifteen sites in the south of the country where large volumes of meltwater form at considerable altitudes (about 1,000 m) and within a short distance of the coast (Fig. 4.1). In western areas there are lakes near the sea which could be used for water storage, but similar facilities do not exist in the south and east of the country. This may mean that in the west power can be generated all year round, whereas in other areas production will be restricted to the summer. Because internal consumption would account for only 5 per cent of Greenland's hydroelectric output, a large surplus would be available for export to North America and Europe, providing difficulties of transmission could be overcome (Partl 1978).

As HEP stations are a fairly recent invention, there is no history of them being overrun by glacier advances. Even so, the tendency for some present-day glaciers to expand raises the question of how soon it will be before installations are damaged or destroyed by ice. Usually, those parts of the system most at risk are the intakes, for as with the old irrigation networks, these have frequently been located near glacier snouts. This hazard may perhaps be avoided by constructing intakes actually beneath the ice, as, for example, in the case of the Argentière glacier, but such an approach has its own particular difficulties (Vivian 1977; Bachmann 1979). If future advances equal or exceed the maxima of the Little Ice Age, not only will intakes be at risk, but also more important structures, like pumping stations and dams (Ch. 8). Indeed, HEP complexes which use significant amounts of glacial meltwater would often best be served by glacier termini remaining at about their present positions. It is far more likely, however, that glacier dimensions will continue to fluctuate, so problems will arise for dependent power stations.

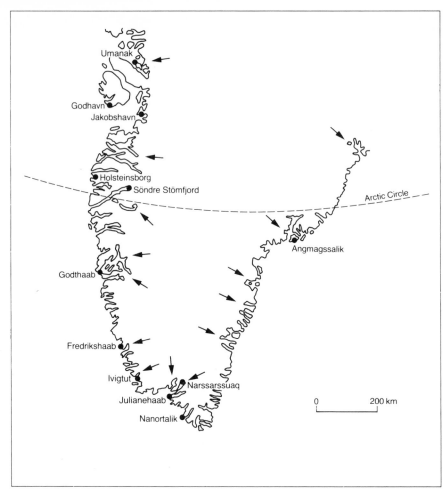

Fig 4.1   Sites in southern Greenland where hydro-electric power might be developed. (After Partl, 1978).

Glacial meltwater can assist the operation of HEP stations by smoothing river discharge. In particular, it can supply plentiful water during hot summers when other sources may dry up. Thus, during the summer of 1947 an extreme drought in eastern Norway caused many streams to vanish, but those fed by glaciers were in spate and so ensured adequate water for power stations which they were supplying (Hoel and Werenskiold 1962).

AGRICULTURE AND FORESTRY

A book published in 1787 describes how flowers and fruit could be picked with one hand, while the other was resting on the ice of the Bossons glacier (Chamonix valley) (Bourrit 1787). About fifty years later a similar reference mentioned an almost ripe ear in a field of rye which first touched the glacier and then withdrew as it swayed in the breeze (Rendu 1840). Such apparent harmony between the glacial and plant king-

Plate 1   Bossons glacier advancing into woodland, August 1981.

doms is, however, the exception, rather than the rule. It would be more appropriate to emphasize that glaciers such as the Bossons have not infrequently destroyed crops, grazing land and trees. Thus, on several occasions during the Little Ice Age (e.g. between 1810 and 1820) this glacier overran fields and woodland (Bourrit 1787; Lyell 1881; Forbes 1900; Grove 1966). A new advance, which began in 1953, has again led to the invasion of woodland by ice (Vivian 1971; 1979; Bachmann 1979) (Plate 1).

The rate at which agricultural land and trees have succumbed to glacial advances has varied. Where the threat has increased gradually, the approach of a glacier front has normally been preceded by climatic decline, which has made plant growth more difficult. Thus, the deterioration associated with nineteenth-century glacier advances in the Karakoram meant that the people of Shigar could obtain only one crop from their fields, whereas previously they were able to grow two (Godwin-Austen 1864). Likewise, the late seventeenth- and eighteenth-century advances of Norwegian glaciers were accompanied by a marked climatic deterioration which led to widespread famine because oats and barley failed to ripen and cattle numbers sharply declined. In the early nineteenth century the Norwegian climate again worsened and glaciers advanced, causing a repeat of previous crop failures and acute starvation (Hoel and Werenskiold 1962; Grove and Battagel 1981). Alpine localities experienced similar problems at various times during the Little Ice Age (Ch. 6; Grove 1966). As a result, in 1703 Hottinger felt obliged to include in his list of evils caused by glaciers the icy winds which blow from them, because these stop fruits and crops maturing (de Beer 1950).

An intriguing problem which emerges from the above remarks and which needs proper investigation is to explain satisfactorily why some crops growing near glaciers reach maturity, though others fail to do so. In this connection it would be interesting to know if the early seventeenth-century glacial maximum, which was primarily caused by temperature decline, had a different impact on crop growth from that of the early

nineteenth century, which was chiefly due to precipitation increase. Equally fasci-
nating would be information on spatial differences in the crop success/failure rates of
areas close to glaciers.

Contrasting with the gradual encroachment of ice on to agricultural and forested
land are the instances of glacier surging which have led to crops, fields and trees being
rapidly overwhelmed. Thus, during the 1720s Engabreen in Norway advanced so
rapidly that it overran crops before they could be harvested (Hoel and Werenskiold
1962; Theakstone 1965; Worsley and Alexander 1976). On another occasion, the
Yengutz glacier in the Karakoram overwhelmed cultivated fields when it rapidly
advanced some 3 km around the turn of the present century (Hayden 1907; Mason
1935; Mercer 1975b). Similar catastrophic destruction of agricultural land and trees
occurred due to an exceptional glacier advance in the Kutiàh valley of the western
Karakoram between March and June 1953 (Desio 1954).

Meltwater streams issuing from glacier fronts have also proved hazardous to
agriculture and trees. The point is well illustrated by fluctuations since about 1820 of
the Austurfljót, a river which emerges from the snout of Hoffellsjökull in Iceland.
While migrating from side to side across its outwash plain (Fig. 4.2), this river has
destroyed fertile meadows. Given the right conditions, however, these may be reconstituted fairly quickly. Thus, in the 1870s the Austurfljót flowed along the eastern
edge of the outwash plain and so destroyed meadows in that area. By around 1910
it had shifted towards the middle of the outwash area, whose eastern parts had therefore recovered sufficiently to be used again for haymaking. This illustrates the
important fact that such outwash plains are basically fertile and if an area is left alone
by meltwater streams it can develop into good grassland within a few decades (Thorarinsson 1956).

Agriculture and forestry are also influenced by the way an advancing glacier erodes
and by the state of the ground exposed through glacial retreat. Observations indicate
that ice can affect the areas over which it moves in a variety of ways. Thus, during
1818 the Le Tour glacier (Chamonix valley) overran 24 m of gravel without ploughing
it up, but when the ice next crossed rather marshy terrain this was 'entirely upraised
and overturned'. At the same time, the nearby Bossons glacier expanded over softish,
arable ground without disturbing it. Indeed, the ice appears to have flowed harmlessly
over almost everything, except mud. Even a bank of soft material which lay in its path
was 'simply crushed, but not eroded' (Collingwood 1884). On the other hand, erosion
was recorded by Lyell (1881), who saw fresh rolls of turf mixed with mud and stones
in the moraines of the Gorner and Findel glaciers (Valais) (Ch. 6). A similar obser-
vation, made in 1823, described the advancing Breidamerkurjökull (Iceland) as
'sweeping the turf in front of it in large rolls, like rolling up cloth'. In this way, much
pasture land was destroyed (Thorarinsson 1943). The generally small amounts of
erosion caused by historic glacier oscillations did not, however, mean that when an
area was deglacierized it could always be speedily returned to agricultural use. On the
contrary, reports frequently complain about the miserable state of ground uncovered
by ice retreat. For example, a manuscript dating from 1663 tells how land exposed
during the previous twenty-five years by retreat of the Chamonix glaciers was still
without grass or cultivation (Blanchard 1913; Ladurie 1967, 1972). Similarly, Forbes
(1900) described terrain uncovered by a withdrawal of the Lys glacier (Italian Alps)
as 'a perfect waste', which is a phrase that could equally apply to many other recently
deglacierized areas. In some cases, land which has succumbed to glacier advances is
never returned to agricultural use. Thus, medieval fields in the Chamonix valley,
which were overrun by Little Ice Age glaciers, are still debris covered (Grove 1966).

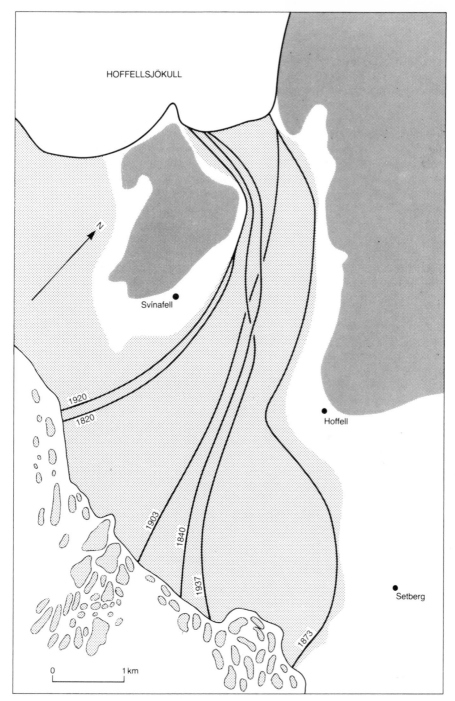

Fig 4.2   The changing course of the glacier river Austurfljót since the beginning of the nineteenth century. (After Thorarinsson, 1956).

The retraction of agricultural limits in this way must have caused great hardships for societies whose mainstay was farming.

Because only rural communities have been affected by the oscillating ice margins of historic times, it is frequently possible to establish a close spatial and temporal relationship between glacier harassment of settlements and that of agricultural land. Hence, references to the former, such as those mentioned in Chapter 3, often contain information on the latter. Even when such information is lacking, it is fairly safe to assume that glaciers which are reported to have damaged or overrun settlements must also have caused problems for the growth of crops and the pasturing of animals. As previously mentioned, societies which did not have recourse to alternative means of sustaining themselves, such as might now be provided by tourism and the import of food, must have viewed nearby glaciers with grave misgivings, knowing the problems they could create.

COMMUNICATIONS AND TRADE

There are, of course, many splendid views in the Alps, but few can be more striking than that presented to southward-bound travellers when they emerge from the dark, fume-laden atmosphere of the Mont Blanc road tunnel to be confronted by the Brenva glacier, its impressive terminus less than 200 m away (Plate 2). Little imagination is needed to appreciate that only a relatively small advance of this terminus would jeopardize the important communications artery which passes through the tunnel. Fortunately, advances of the Brenva terminus which occurred during the 1970s were not sufficient to bring the ice up against the embankment on which the road is build. The existence of a lateral moraine near the tunnel mouth is, however, a reminder that several times previously the Brenva has reached and even gone beyond the embankment (Müller 1977; Vivian 1979). Another road which would be threatened by a growth of Brenva ice is that which passes the chapel of Notre Dame de la Guérison (Ch. 3) on its way up the Val Veni to the Miage glacier (Plate 3). Though less important than the Mont Blanc tunnel route, this nevertheless provides access to a beautiful and much-frequented Alpine valley. When Captain Hall toured the area in 1818 he found a road which had been deliberately sited well above the valley floor to avoid the glacier. By the time of his visit, however, the ice had thickened so much that it had risen to the level of the road and partly destroyed it. In addition, Hall saw a path which was cut by the glacier, but which was plainly visible on either side of the ice (Hall 1841).

The dangers currently posed by the Brenva are merely among the latest in a long history of encounters between glaciers and communications in the Alps. Such encounters were numerous during the Little Ice Age when glaciers extended towards inhabited areas and highlevel col routes. Examples of the former situation have occurred in the Chamonix valley, where the Bossons glacier, Mer de Glace and Argentière glacier became threatening to communications. Thus, in 1644 the Mer de Glace descended so far into the valley that people feared it might block the Arve river (Ladurie 1967, 1972). If this were to happen again, the main road and rail communications along the valley would almost certainly be cut at Les Tines. Fortunately, even during the maxima of the Little Ice Age, relatively few glaciers encroached upon areas of habitation as important as the Chamonix valley. Many, however, did interfere with high-level communication routes, which had been developed during the climatically favourable years of the medieval period as links between peoples on the

Plate 2   Terminus of the Brenva glacier from near the entrance to the Mont Blanc road tunnel.

Plate 3   Brenva glacier and road from the chapel of Notre Dame de la Guérison.

opposing sides of a watershed. Not infrequently, these high-level passes had enabled economically contrasting communities to become mutually dependent. Glacier expansion during the Little Ice Age therefore seriously disrupted the economic life of some communities, as it first increased the difficulty of maintaining links with nearby valleys and then severed those links completely (Ch. 6). The hazard persisted at various Alpine localities throughout the Little Ice Age and was still causing problems in the

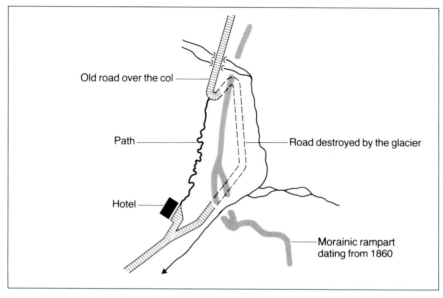

Fig 4.3   The partial destruction of the old road over the Susten pass due to the nineteenth century advances of the Stein glacier. (After Bachmann, 1979).

mid nineteenth century. It has been suggested, for example, that there are few early references to the Susten pass because the Little Ice Age expansion of the Stein glacier made the route difficult or even impossible (de Beer 1967). Certainly, this glacier was still large enough in 1860 to be covering a part of the road (Fig. 4.3)(Bachmann 1979).

Although it is possible to cite many examples of Alpine glaciers which have inter-fered with communications and trade, there are other mountain ranges where the problem has been more serious. For instance, glaciers in the Caucasus have been a major harassment and even a barrier to communications and have therefore helped to separate different communities. The central Caucasus, which is the worst affected part of the range, has only one road crossing the mountains that is not threatened by ice and so does not require the use of tunnels. Other important routes (e.g. that at Klukhorskiy Pereval in the western Caucasus) pass close enough to glaciers for them to be cut were a significant expansion of ice to occur. In view of the general situation, it is hardly surprising that many north–south journeys across the Caucasus involve traversing glacier passes (Horvath and Field 1975).

Karakoram glaciers, like those of the Caucasus, have presented major difficulties for trade and communications (Horvath and Field 1975). Especially interesting are the examples of mountain routes which were harassed or closed by ice near the end of or even after the Little Ice Age. Thus, trade links across the Baltoro glacier and Mustagh pass, which had been practicable in the early 1800s, were abandoned in the mid nineteenth century due to a marked glacier advance and increase of snow. Like-wise, between 1855 and 1861 the Panmah glacier expanded and overran a road together with bushes and trees. Also during the 1860s, the Chong Kumdan and Kickik Kumdan interfered with communications. In 1902–3, after a rapid advance, the latter again barred the route up the Shyok valley where road building had started about four years earlier. The problem was aggravated by thrusts of the Aktash glacier in 1905 and of the Chong Kumdan in 1909, so that ice eventually blocked the road in three places (Godwin–Austen 1864; Longstaff 1910; Mason 1929; Mercer 1975b).

Rather similar difficulties have been experienced in modern times with the recently built Karakoram Highway. First, in 1974, meltwater from the Batura glacier destroyed a bridge on the Highway and then, in 1980, the road was cut by water and debris from the Ghulkin glacier (Derbyshire and Miller 1981; Goudie 1981).

The examples quoted show that during the last 130 years Karakoram glaciers have continued to be an important hazard for trade and communications, whereas in the Alps the problem has undergone a rather significant reduction over the same period. This is partly due to the glaciers themselves, for it appears that even today Karakoram passes contain more ice than they did at the end of the eighteenth century (the use of many routes within the area still necessitates travelling over glaciers) (Mercer 1975b). It is partly also because some roads in the Karakoram have been built near to glaciers (e.g. sections of the modern Karakoram Highway). Unfortunately, this type of difficulty cannot always be avoided owing to the restrictive nature of Kara- koram valleys. To site the Highway further from the Ghulkin glacier would, in fact, mean two extra bridgings of the Hunza river and the building of a new road across extensive and steep talus cones (Derbyshire and Miller 1981).

Although glaciers have hindered trade and communications in regions such as the Alps, Caucasus and Karakoram, it would be wrong to assume that they have necess- arily been troublesome in other mountain areas. There is, for instance, no history of them having any direct influence as barriers or routeways in the Canadian Rockies (Denton 1975a). It would also be incorrect to assume that only the glacier fluctuations of mountain regions have affected trade and communications. Lowland ice may also create difficulties as, for example, in the Austur–Skaftafellssýsla region of southern Iceland, where journeys between farms have sometimes involved the crossing of glacier snouts (Thorarinsson 1960). More importantly, the coast road from southern to eastern Iceland has often been plagued by advances of the Breidamerkurjökull (Ahlmann and Thorarinsson 1937; Thorarinsson 1943). Croot and Escritt (1976) put the problem into a modern setting with their photograph of a road bridge which was opened in 1974 across the outwash plains south of Vatnajökull and which is at risk from glacier outbursts and advances. Tradition maintains that there have also been at least two routes by which people actually crossed the Vatnajökull ice-cap in a north–south direction. One of these, which joined northern Iceland with the fishing grounds off Kálfafellsstadur, was abandoned probably in 1575 after a tragic accident at sea. The other, which is said to have been for taking wood to northern regions where it was unobtainable, had fallen into disuse by the end of the eighteenth century owing to the difficulty of crossing the ice (Ahlmann and Thorarinsson 1937). In the same way, routes have for centuries crossed the glaciers of Norway. Traditionally, these served to link communities, foster trade and promote religious contacts: in more recent times, many have acquired a new importance as tourist routes. The history of tracks across Folgefonni, Jostedalsbreen, Jotunheimen, Flatkjølen and Lappfjellet has been outlined by Hoel and Werenskiold (1962). Similarly, Grant and Higgins (1913) mention that the Valdez glacier (Alaska) was much used as a routeway during 1898–99 by those seeking gold in the Copper River and Yukon basins, while a track over the Portage glacier was for more than a century frequented first by traders and then by miners travelling from Prince William Sound to Cook Inlet.

MINING

Advancing glaciers can hinder mining operations in two main ways. First, they can affect communications linking the place of extraction with the destination of the material, and secondly, they can overrun the extraction site itself. Unfortunately, the past importance of these hindrances is sometimes difficult to assess. This is partly because a number of stories exist which have yet to be verified. For example, it is reputed that medieval silver mines (now ice covered) occur near Argentière in the Chamonix valley. Though the name of this village is apparently derived from the French word for silver, no one has yet proved that such mines existed (Bourrit 1787; Matthes 1942; Ladurie 1967, 1972). Further problems of interpretation arise owing to the difficulties of separating glacial from non-glacial influences. In Austria, for example, glaciers undoubtedly contributed to the decline of high-altitude mining in the late sixteenth and seventeenth centuries, though other factors were also important. Thus, the decline of gold mining in the Rauris and Gastein valleys (Salzburg Alps) was due to glacier advance plus the longer and more severe winters, all of which increasingly caused mine entrances to be blocked by ice and snow (Schwarzl 1979). Where recent glacier shrinkage has uncovered evidence of former mining activity, it is tempting to believe claims that other mine workings exist beneath the ice. One such claim maintains that further shrinkage is required before the Pasterze glacier (Gross-glockner region) uncovers all of the mines which it overran during the advances of the Little Ice Age (Péguy 1956). Difficulties also exist with some of the South American evidence. For example, there have been several articles describing how former mining sites in the Ananea region of south-eastern Peru were re-exposed by glacier shrinkage around 1900, though the information given has not been wholly consistent (Hastenrath 1981).

While no serious inquiry into the effects of glaciers on mining can ignore the types of problem outlined above, it would be wrong to give the impression that the topic is riddled with uncertainty. There is, for example, indisputable evidence that glaciers once threatened the Copper River and Northwestern Railroad (Alaska), which was constructed between 1906 and 1910 to link the Kennicott Copper Mines with the port of Cordova. Along one 50 km stretch in the coastal Chugach Mountains the railroad had to pass close by six glaciers where they debouched into the main valley. During the later stages of construction work two of the glaciers surged. By 1911 one of them (the Childs glacier) had advanced to within 450 m of the so-called Miles Glacier Bridge, a structure which cost $1,500,000. The Kennicott Mine was, however, abandoned in the late 1930s and eventually had its rail link superseded by a highway. As if to show the versatility of nature's armoury, this was extensively damaged by the earthquake of 1964 (Field 1975b).

The modern search for resources has not surprisingly led to the finding of deposits close to or even beneath glaciers. In such cases there are often formidable problems if extraction is to be undertaken successfully. Typical are the difficulties examined in a feasibility study carried out at Isua on the south-western edges of the Greenland ice sheet. This area possesses an iron-ore deposit 2 km long and 250–450 m wide, most of which lies beneath up to 200 m of ice. In order to expose the ore for open-pit mining, it would initially be necessary to excavate 172×10^6 m^3 of ice. A further 7.9 $\times 10^6$ m^3 would then have to be removed annually as the glacier flowed towards the operations site. Because the life of the mine could exceed thirty years (Colbeck 1974), there is presumably a likelihood that work there might be affected by glacier variations. Similar problems will doubtless be encountered when attempts are made to exploit the mineral resources of Antarctica.

TOURISM AND RECREATION

In mountain regions such as the Alps and Caucasus, which are accessible to large numbers of people, glaciers have become features of tourist and recreational interest (Horvath and Field 1975; Mercer 1975a; Vivian 1977; Bachmann 1979). This interest probably had its beginnings in June 1741 when two Englishmen, Windham and Pococke, visited the Mer de Glace and one of them afterwards published an account of their experiences (de Beer 1967; Vivian 1976; Bachmann 1979). Today, this glacier system is among the most popular in the world. During 1975 the railway which takes visitors from Chamonix to Montenvers, where they can see the famous S-bend shape of the Mer de Glace, carried the equivalent of 400,000 passengers on both the outward and return journey. Over the same period no less than 640,000 visits were recorded at the Aiguille du Midi cable-car station, from which there is a splendid view of the Vallée Blanche part of the Mer de Glace system (Vivian 1976). Although this system continues to provide some of the most breathtaking landscapes in the western Alps. ice shrinkage must have diminished the splendour of the scene relative to that which greeted Windham and Pococke in 1741. This fact is a reminder that the significance of glaciers as objects of tourist and recreational interest is affected by fluctuations in their extent. One can, indeed, think of glaciers as having an optimum size which enables them to provide the maximum benefits for the visitor without being noticeably detrimental to other aspects of the local economy. Thus, scenery and tourism in the Chamonix valley would be poorer were the snouts of the Le Tour and Argentière glaciers to retreat a short distance and vanish from the gaze of tourists in the valley bottom. Equally, cameras would not click so busily in the centre of Chamonix were the long tongue of the Bossons glacier to become severely truncated. On the other hand, Chamoniards would also be unhappy if glaciers began returning to maximum Little Ice Age positions, thereby interfering with fields, settlements, communications and the various trappings of the tourist industry. It is perhaps ironic that, having broken their dependence on high-altitude farming, Chamoniards have become reliant on tourism, for this too is a livelihood affected by the vagaries of the weather and the fluctuations of glaciers. The problem is a familiar one in many high-mountain localities.

CHAPTER 5
GLACIER FLOODS AND ICE AVALANCHES

When discussing glacier hazards, it is convenient to examine separately glacier floods and ice avalanches. The violence displayed by these phenomena contrasts sharply with the more gradual events typical of fluctuations in the extent and thickness of glaciers. As a result, their impact on the human and natural worlds has been greater. Usually, this impact is more pronounced when glaciers are advancing, rather than retreating.

GLACIER FLOODS

Origins

Glacier floods (also known as *débâcles, jökulhlaups*, or glacier outbursts) can arise for a variety of reasons. In some cases they are due to the rapid escape of water which has been impounded behind a dam of ice and, perhaps, moraine. The events leading to this type of flood may begin when climatic deterioration induces a side-valley glacier to expand towards the main valley at a point where this is ice-free. If the junction between the two valleys is markedly discordant, ice may break away from the terminus of the expanding glacier, avalanche into the principal valley and form a regenerated (reconstituted) glacier at some distance from the parent ice body. Such glaciers are now less common in the Alps than they were during the nineteenth century (Mercer 1975a), though many still occur in Norway (Vanni 1966). Some (e.g. that currently being formed below the Le Tour glacier) pose no threat to river flow in the principal valley, whereas others (e.g the regenerated Little Ice Age Giétro glacier) may interfere to such an extent that water becomes impounded by the ice to form a lake. Since the ice tends to be poorly consolidated, there is always the danger that lake water will break free and inundate areas downvalley with catastrophic results. Striking examples of this occurred in 1595 and 1818, due to outbursts caused by the Giétro glacier (see Chs 6 and 7).

When the junction between a main valley and its tributary is essentially accordant, there is little chance that a regenerated glacier will develop. Instead, the ice will expand without a significant interruption or breakage towards the main valley where it will probably spread into a lobate form. Initially at least, the stream in the principal valley may find its way round or beneath the ice, a situation which occurred a number of times during the first half of the nineteenth century when side-valley glaciers (e.g. the Breney and Mont Durand) advanced into the Val de Bagnes (Valais). According to Forbes (1900), streams can more easily maintain an open channel beneath a glacier which is advancing in this way than when they are invaded by falling ice. Mason (1929), on the other hand, has pointed out that during winter such a river would be frozen and without erosive power, so that a blockage might well occur. It is therefore not difficult to find instances of glaciers which have advanced into a main valley, barred its stream and caused a lake to form behind their dam of ice and moraine. Although such dams are usually firmer than those provided by regenerated glaciers, they have not infrequently allowed the violent escape of much lake water, sometimes on a repeated basis and with disastrous results. The Vernagt glacier (Ötztal Alps) is a good example, having caused serious *débâcles* in 1600, 1678, 1680, 1773, 1845, 1847 and 1848 (Fig. 5.1) (Ladurie 1967, 1972; Hoinkes 1969).

Sometimes, ice-dammed lakes form due to glacier sliding. This process is 'intermediate' between the two just described, as it involves rapid forward movement of ice and blocking of rivers, though without the element of free fall which characterizes the Giétro-type situation. Large-scale movements of this kind have been observed in the Andes, but not in the Alps. They develop when a tributary of white névé–ice rests on top of a darker trunk glacier, rather than the two existing side by side. As tributary glaciers are broken into pinnacles, traversed by crevasses and overlie a moving surface of darker ice, they are rather unstable features. Processes which can set them in motion include heavy precipitation, avalanches, and increased meltwater production during hot weather. These may cause displacement along shear planes roughly parallel to the base of the white névé–ice. In Argentina movements of this sort occurred during the early 1930s when a marked thrust of névé–ice over the Nevado glacier and then downvalley led to blocking of the Rio Plomo. The lake which formed was violently evacuated in 1934 with catastrophic results (King 1934; Helbling 1935; Haefeli 1966).

If a main valley is occupied by a glacier, lakes may form in its ice-free tributaries. The most famous example is probably the Märjelensee in Switzerland (Chs 6 and 7). though such features are actually better developed in Iceland (Thorarinsson 1939, 1956), Norway (Liestøl 1955) and Alaska (Stone 1963). While there is rarely any likelihood of the ice barrier giving way under the pressure of lake water, violent outbursts can still occur. These tend to arise when water rapidly escapes through or under the ice dam, its passage being aided by the existence of crevasses and other openings within or beneath the glacier. Such events can cause an ice-dammed lake to be totally drained. In some cases (e.g. Øvre Mjølkedalsvatn in Norway; Liestøl 1955), water may flow away over a nearby col, thus restricting lake growth and permitting an essentially noncatastrophic discharge in roughly the opposite direction to any sub-or englacial escape. Less frequently, the partial draining of lake water may occur over the ice surface. Because of these various means of lake discharge, water-level in such features is characterized by numerous and often rapid changes which may lead to flooding that extends many kilometres downvalley.

Glacier lakes can also form at the junction of valleys. Forbes (1900) has described one such type which develops in the angle between two confluent glaciers, especially when melting is rapid. He quoted as an example a lake at the junction of the Tacul and Leschaux glaciers in the Mont Blanc range. Variations of lake level suggested to Forbes that water was being discharged underneath the glacier and that this was probably one explanation for sudden rises of the Arveyron river. However, due to the present contracted state of glaciers, this lake is now dry (Vivian 1976; Bachmann 1979). Another possibility is that during a period of retreat two glaciers which once had a common tongue will separate and thereafter contract at different rates. Meltwater from the more rapidly shrinking glacier may become dammed by the ice

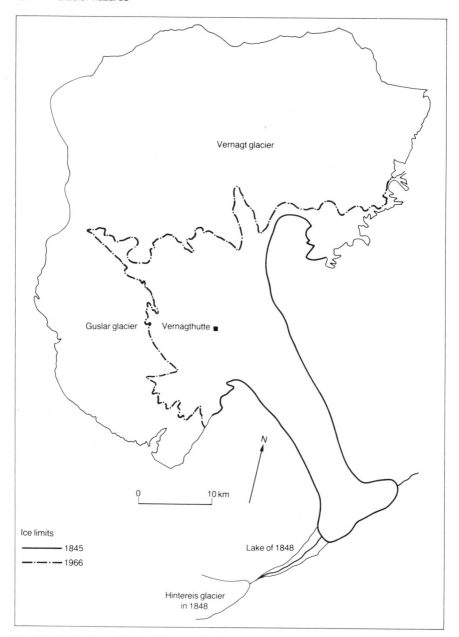

Fig 5.1 Fluctuations of the Vernagt and Guslar glaciers together with the position of the ice-dammed lake of 1848. (After Hoinkes, 1969).

and moraine of the more slowly retreating tongue, thus forming a lake. This may periodically discharge and cause flooding downvalley.

When a glacier is retreating, small lakes may begin to develop on the ice tongue. As shrinkage continues, these may coalesce to form a large body of supra-/proglacial water. Although this water is often in contact with the ice front, it is actually held in place by the occurrence downstream of a terminal moraine or because it occupies a depression in the outwash area. Frontal lakes of this sort are well developed in the Cordillera Blanca of Peru. About 230 are found there and some have emptied violently, causing great damage and loss of life. Water may discharge through or over a moraine and can be set in motion by ice calving into the lake and generating destructive waves (Rüegg 1962; Lliboutry 1971, 1973; Lliboutry *et al.* 1977).

Débâcles can also originate in lakes and water pockets which form on, within or beneath a glacier. For example, if meltwater is unable to escape by the usual routes, a build-up may occur and a lake may develop on the ice surface. The collapse of voids within or beneath a glacier may also promote lake formation by creating ice surface irregularities in which water can accumulate. Likewise, en- and subglacial water pockets may constitute a danger, as when in 1892 a catastrophic *débâcle* poured out from the Tête Rousse glacier in the French Alps. Observations indicate that pockets of meltwater became impounded within the ice at a point where the glacier was passing over a rock sill in the valley long profile. Eventually, the pressure of water which had accumulated (about 200,000 m³) became such that the ice barrier gave way and a violent *débâcle* ensued (Vivian 1974, 1979; Preusser 1976; Bachmann 1979).

When ice and fire meet, considerable volumes of meltwater are produced and the results may be disastrous for people and property. Iceland is a classic locality for this type of *débâcle*. Although the emptying of glacier-dammed lakes is the most frequent cause of Icelandic *jökulhlaups*, outbursts produced by volcanic activity tend to be much more destructive. In some cases, vulcanicity occurs subglacially and melts the ice from below. On other occasions, the eruption is near a glacier and its effects are sufficiently widespread for appreciable volumes of ice to be melted. The Grimsvötn volcano, which lies beneath Vatnajökull, is perhaps the best-known source of *jökulhlaups* in Iceland. This volcano forms a huge depression which gets filled with meltwater produced by surface ablation and solfataric activity underneath the ice. When a critical volume of meltwater has accumulated in the depression a violent *jökulhlaup* occurs and the flood penetrates some 50 km through the ice to emerge at Skeidarársandur. Often (though not invariably) the Grimsvötn *jökulhlaups* have been accompanied by a volcanic eruption which is probably triggered off due to the sudden release of water pressure (Thorarinsson 1956; Preusser 1976; Paterson 1981).

Finally, some *débâcles* have occurred when rock and debris has fallen on to a glacier from nearby slopes and has consequently mixed with and expelled water from the ice or its immediate surroundings. A repetitive and destructive happening of this sort has plagued the Dents du Midi–Bois Noir area of Valais. On one such occasion (26 August 1835), the day after a violent storm, there was a rock fall from the Dents du Midi on to a neighbouring glacier. The ice–water–debris mixture thereby produced then entered the St Barthélemy torrent and had its water content so increased that it descended to the Rhône river at Bois Noir like a stream of lava. Other mudflows occurred shortly afterwards and together they caused much destruction and interrupted communications in the Rhône valley (Lardy 1836; Montandon 1926; Mariétan 1927b; Tufnell 1980).

Climatic and glacier fluctuations obviously play a major role in the formation of *débâcles*. Sometimes, however, non-glacial factors (e.g. vulcanicity or mass movements) are important. Even so, these do not necessarily escape the influence of climatic and glacier changes. For example, since 1934 Grimsvötn *jökulhlaups* have decreased in volume, but increased in frequency as the thickness of ice overlying the volcanic area has diminished (Preusser 1976).

Frequency and magnitude

A study of more than fifty well-known *débâcles* in the Alps has shown that over 95 per cent occurred in the months of June to September inclusive. Within this period there were two maxima, June and August. The first seems largely attributable to floods caused by variations in glacier length, while the second appears due to the rupture of water pockets within the ice (Vivian 1974). Research elsewhere has broadly supported these views on the seasonal timing of *débâcles*. For example, in Washington State, USA, glacier *débâcles* occur in late summer and autumn, whereas floods due to heavy precipitation are a winter phenomenon (Richardson 1968). Similarly, Liestøl (1955) has pointed out that, because of the way physical processes operate, glacial lakes will usually empty in summer or early autumn. It has, however, been observed that the timing of *débâcles* within the June–September period may vary over the years. In 1898 a glacier lake in Vatnsdalur (Iceland) started to drain annually, but over the next forty years the time of emptying gradually became earlier. Around the turn of the century it used to be in late September, whereas by 1938 it had advanced to early July (Thorarinsson 1939).

Although summer–early autumn is the preferred season for glacier *débâcles*, they have occasionally happened at other times of the year. Thus, Liestøl (1955) points out that Mjølkedalsvatn in Norway has emptied in midwinter and early spring, while Vivian (1974) notes that winter *débâcles* have sometimes occurred in the western Alps. When examined on a yearly basis, the periodicity of Alpine *débâcles* was found to be of three broad types (Vivian 1974). First, some outbursts take place annually or even several times a year. In the western Alps these have been especially associated with lakes which develop at the confluence of retreating glaciers (e.g. the Gorner lake in Valais: Ch. 6). Secondly, there are *débâcles* which have occurred irregularly over a time-scale of many years. These have been particularly associated with barrier lakes, such as were formed by the Allalin (Chs 6 and 7), Vernagt and Rutor glaciers. Outside of the Alps, this type of periodicity has been exhibited by volcanic *jökulhlaups*. Finally, some *débâcles* (e.g. certain of those due to the formation of intraglacial water pockets) appear to be rather isolated phenomena (e.g. the Tête Rousse disaster of 1892) caused by a special combination of circumstances.

The frequency of *débâcles* at a particular locality can vary over the years. This is because the processes causing them are not static, but fluctuate according to the condition of glaciers and other environmental phenomena. Thus, the devastating series of outbursts in the Cordillera Blanca of Peru began only after a widespread glacier recession set in during the 1920s (Lliboutry *et al.* 1977). Similarly, it has been proposed that Alaskan ice-dammed lakes develop in four stages, each of which is marked by changes in the periodicity of lake emptying (Stone 1963).

The magnitude of *débâcles*, like their frequency, can be very variable. According to Lliboutry (1971), the largest outbursts of subglacial water tend to be the volcanic *jökulhlaups* of Iceland. Thorarinsson (1956) has pointed out that the Grimsvötn floods produce a maximum runoff of about 50,000 m³/second, which is a rate of flow 1,000 times greater than that of the Thames at low water. Twice as large again or more were peak flows for the *jökulhlaups* of 1918 in the Katla area and 1362 in Öraefi. It has, however, been shown that Katla *jökulhlaups* differ from many others in Iceland because their maximum runoff is very high relative to the total amount of water discharged (Thorarinsson 1957, 1958). Significantly lower are maximum flow values for outbursts caused by the emptying of ice-dammed lakes. For example, the catastrophic Vatnsdalur *jökulhlaup* of 1898 achieved a maximum runoff of only 3,000 m³/second, while the 1939 outburst from Graenalón, the largest glacier lake in

Iceland, managed a peak flow of 6,000 m³/second. On the other hand, the *volume* of water discharged in the Graenalón flood was only one-quarter less than would be released in a Katla-type outburst with a peak flow of 200,000 m³/second (Thorarinsson 1939, 1956, 1957). The discharge rates for other Icelandic *jökulhlaups* have been tabulated by Preusser (1976).

Especially in recent decades, attempts have been made to control or even remove the dangers posed by glacier *débâcles*. An example of this is the work carried out by the Peruvians in the Cordillera Blanca (Lliboutry *et al.* 1977) (see Ch. 7 for Swiss responses to the problem). Mankind is therefore exerting an increasing influence on the character of glacier *débâcles*.

Impact

Débâcles probably constitute a more serious threat to mankind than do other glacier hazards, for they have a history not only of destroying property, but also of causing injury and death to people as well as animals and plants. In addition, they can have substantial geomorphological effects and often extend their havoc much further beyond the edges of ice-covered areas than do other glacier hazards. When assessing the impact of some *débâcles*, it is necessary to recognize the prior effects of the ice-dammed lakes from which they originated. Thus, in 1942 the Moreno glacier (Argentina) was impounding water in the Lago Rico area to such an extent that a large expanse of agricultural land became flooded. Rises in lake level have also killed many trees and have deposited sand and mud which was inimical to ground vegetation. A number of small buildings have been destroyed by waves and floating wood from the lake (Nichols and Miller 1952).

Hazards of this sort are, of course, rather unimportant when measured against the dangers posed by violent glacier floods. Nowhere has this been more forcibly demonstrated than in the Cordillera Blanca of Peru. The earliest known glacier flood in this region dates from 1725 and is thought to have killed between 1,500 and 2,000 people in the village of Ancash. Thereafter, no more floods of this nature occurred in the area until the 1930s, when two unimportant *débâcles* initiated what was to become a devastating series of glacier tragedies. The first of these, in 1941, was caused by an outburst from Laguna de Palcacocha which destroyed one-third of the city of Huaraz and killed over 6,000 people. At least it prompted the setting up of a commission to try and reduce the problem. Even so, another tragedy struck in 1945 when an outburst from Quebrada Huachescsa destroyed the ancient town of Chavin de Huantar, leaving many dead. Then, in 1950, while engineering work was actually in progress, there was an outburst from Laguna Jancarurish, which may have killed as many as 500 people. Fortunately, more recent *débâcles* in the Cordillera Blanca have had only a small impact on the local population (Lliboutry 1971, 1973; Lliboutry *et al.* 1977).

An outburst which appears to have matched the severity of those in the Cordillera Blanca has been reported by Vivian (1979). He was told by a lama that in 1953 several thousand people were killed when ice from a Tibetan glacier fell into a proglacial lake and generated a disastrous flood. By contrast, the death toll in the worst Alpine *débâcles* has been much less. The Tête Rousse disaster of 1892 claimed only 177 lives, many of whom were at the baths of St Gervais (Lliboutry 1971; Bachmann 1979; Vivian 1979). Slightly less disastrous was the Giétro outburst of 1595 which killed about 150 people (Ch. 6). Glacier floods are also known to have damaged or destroyed settlements and caused loss of life in the Karakoram (Godwin-Austen 1864; Mason 1929; Finsterwalder 1960), Argentina (King 1934; Bachmann 1979), Iceland

(Eythorsson 1935; Thorarinsson 1939, 1943, 1956, 1958), Norway (Liestøl 1955) and Alaska (Stone 1963).

In some cases, the effects of glacier *débâcles* on settlement are relatively short-lived – the mud and debris have been cleared away from around the baths at St Gervais and some of the buildings which were destroyed have been re-erected, so that medical facilities continue to be offered at the centre. On the other hand, *débâcles* can have a much more serious and protracted effect. Thus, Thorarinsson (1956) has pointed out that in the Austur–Skaftafellssýsla district of Iceland they have had a profound and long-lasting influence on settlement in two main ways. First, they have caused it to move from the plains to the comparative security of elevated ground, and secondly they are responsible for the clustering of farms, such as is found in Öraefi. This latter situation has come about because glacier rivers and *jökulhlaups* have reduced the area of habitable land. Rather than move elsewhere, the people decided to bring their farms together, so they could help each other to cultivate the land which was left.

This example shows that *débâcles* can affect not only population and settlement, but also agriculture. A major reason for this is that they often rapidly accomplish large amounts of geomorphological work. In this connection it is significant that the terms *aluvión* and *huayco*, which are used in Peru, refer to floods not of clear water, but of liquid mud (Lliboutry *et al.* 1977). Therefore, the Jancarurish outburst of 1950, which released 2 million m³ of water, carried with it 3 million m³ of sediment. Likewise, in France the Tête Rousse *débâcle* of 1892 brought down 800,000 m³ of sediment in only 200,000 m³ of water (Lliboutry 1971; Vivian 1974; Bachmann 1979). Though *débâcles* often erode large amounts of agriculturally unproductive land, they also frequently remove valuable topsoil, as with many of the Icelandic examples. Nevertheless, certain environmental conditions will limit their erosive ability. For instance, the big 1898 outburst from Vatnsdalur removed little soil because the ground was frozen (Thorarinsson 1939, 1956). *Débâcles* may also ruin crops, destroy farm buildings and kill farm animals, as happened in the Shyok glacier floods of 1835 and 1926. These are also noteworthy because they show that the hazard can be effective many kilometres from its source. Thus, the 1926 outburst destroyed the village of Abadan together with its cultivated land, even though these were 400 km downstream from where the flood originated (Mason 1929).

The peak flows achieved by *débâcles* can rise many metres above normal river level, especially within the confines of a gorge. During the 1926 Shyok outburst there was an increase of 21 m over normal flood level in the gorges between Unmaru and Biagdangdo, which are 300 km from where the *débâcle* originated (Mason 1929). Similarly, the Tête Rousse flood of 1892 rose almost to the height of the Pont du Diable (Devil's Bridge), which crosses the narrow Bonnant gorge 62 m above normal river level (Bachmann 1979). In many cases, however, bridges which lie in the track of such rapidly moving and swollen torrents do not escape injury or destruction (Mason 1929, 1935; Thorarinsson 1939; Liestøl 1955; Finsterwalder 1960; Stone 1963; Richardson 1968). Hence, the disruption to communications may be severe, as in 1845 when a flood from the Rofensee destroyed eighteen out of twenty-one bridges in the Ötztal (Bachmann 1979). The frequent need for roads and railways to bridge streams therefore puts them at risk from glacier *débâcles*. Consequently, it is not surprising that this was the hazard which first caused people to study glacier-dammed lakes in Alaska (Stone 1963). *Débâcles* at the Spiral Tunnels (British Columbia) have highlighted two aspects of the problem. First, they have shown the need to protect communication routes, especially where the hazard develops repeatedly (at this locality destructive glacier outbursts occurred in 1925, 1946 and 1978). Secondly, they have demonstrated that outbursts can sweep away moving traffic, as well as road and railway structures (the 1978 event not only damaged the Canadian Pacific Railroad and the Trans-Canada Highway, but also derailed a freight train) (Jackson 1979).

ICE AVALANCHES

Characteristics and origins

During the Little Ice Age, when glaciers expanded, ice avalanches were probably a more serious hazard than they are today, because a larger proportion of them occurred near inhabited areas. This does not necessarily mean that their overall frequency was greater during that period. Unfortunately, it is impossible to determine how the situation has varied over time, since widespread and comprehensive observations of ice avalanche events have never been made. People therefore have somewhat different views on the frequency of such phenomena. Heybrock (1935), for example, thinks ice avalanches are comparatively rare, while Vivian (1979) feels that they are not particularly unusual. The problem is further complicated by ice avalanches occurring at different frequencies and magnitudes in different areas. Thus, Heybrock (1935) claims that such features are of much greater size in the central Caucasus than in the Alps. Likewise, the many summer avalanches which originate at the front of the Le Tour glacier (Chamonix valley) usually involve only small amounts of material (Plate 4), whereas ice totalling millions of cubic metres was set in motion by the large glacier avalanches of 1895 (Altels), 1962 (Huascarán) and 1965 (Allalin: Chs 6 and 7). The

Plate 4   Le Tour glacier from the village of Le Tour. The whiter parts of the regenerated glacier are due to an ice fall on 15 August 1981.

volume of an avalanche may be greatly increased by debris and river water which becomes incorporated into the moving mass. This is most likely to happen when an avalanche travels well beyond the margins of its glacier. A classic example is provided by the terrible Huascaràn disaster of 1962, for what began as a displacement of up to 3 million m³ of ice was transformed on its downhill journey into a mudflow totalling 13 million m³. The maximum velocity attained by this mass (over 100 km/hour) is some indication of the extremes which can occur with this type of glacier hazard, though it has to be said that the 1970 Huascaràn disaster, which was a more complex and deadly event, achieved speeds up to four times greater. Because of such rapid motion, it is hardly surprising that blocks of ice are quickly pulverized and may even be transformed into water, as happened during the 1962 Huascaràn disaster (Morales 1966; Lliboutry 1971, 1975; Röthlisberger 1977). In 1819, a mass of ice which broke away from the Bies glacier (Valais) underwent such pulverization that it was turned into an airborne-powder avalanche. Furthermore, the wind associated with it did immense damage to the village of Randa (Ch. 6). Although several important avalanches have originated from the Bies glacier (Table 6.7, p. 72), none has travelled more than a short distance beyond the edge of the ice. In spite of this, some geomorphological work was accomplished. The ice and debris cones which these avalanches produced did not, however, give rise to regenerated glaciers, such as have been developed by the Le Tour and Balmes glaciers in the French Alps (Vivian 1979). At some localities, the tracks and run-out zones of ice avalanches will fail to exceed the limits of their parent glacier, in which case they may simply be reincorporated into the ice (Röthlisberger 1977). This is more likely to occur in the Caucasus than in the Alps, because glaciers in the former area occupy valleys with gentle long profiles, so that ice avalanches tend to occur near their heads; by contrast, Alpine glaciers are more likely to terminate on steep rocky slopes which is where many of their ice avalanches originate (Heybrock 1935).

In an attempt to distinguish various types of ice avalanche, Haefeli (1966) has proposed several criteria (nature of the rupture, type of movement, etc.) which might form the basis of a classification. He has also mentioned that the problem of differentiating between ice avalanches and very pronounced glacier thrusts may be clarified by recognizing that only in the former case does the moving ice totally separate from its parent glacier. The mechanisms whereby separation can occur are of two main kinds – some avalanches develop by calving and free fall from a hanging glacier, while others involve the detachment and sliding of tabular masses of ice. In both cases, avalanching may be of either the full depth or the surface (i.e. partial depth) variety. As shown by Röthlisberger (1977), the processes giving rise to ice avalanches can be elucidated through the careful study of those instances which have been relatively well documented. Although such avalanches are each developed and triggered by a unique combination of factors, their origins often have things in common, for they all relate to the basic problem of ice stability on a steep incline. Glacier flow patterns and crevasse development are particularly useful indicators when trying to forecast ice avalanches. Climate obviously has a dominant influence on the build-up and release of such features, but the role of earth movements is less certain. For many years, earthquakes were thought to be a significant cause of glacier surges and ice avalanches (e.g. Heybrock 1935), but events such as the severe Alaskan earthquake of 1964 appear to have refuted this theory (Eckel 1970). On the other hand, the 1970 Huascaràn disaster, though not caused by a true glacier avalanche, did involve the movement of large volumes of ice and was triggered off by a major earthquake. Further clarification of the problem is obviously required.

Impact

Despite their violence, ice avalanches are a less serious hazard than glacier *débâcles* and are nowhere near as important as earthquakes or traffic accidents. This is largely because they often fail to extend their influence much beyond glacier margins and are therefore not particularly successful in penetrating inhabited areas. Certainly, they are less common in mountain valleys than are snow avalanches and this, not surprisingly, means that they are also less well understood. Furthermore, they are harder to control, so that on the few occasions when they do make contact with populated areas their impact tends to be considerable, especially as it will probably have been unalleviated by defensive measures (Röthlisberger 1977). Also significant is the growth of recreation in high-mountain localities, for this is putting a small, but increasing number of people at risk from both snow and ice avalanches. Whereas skiers are the chief group affected by snow avalanches, it is climbers who are most likely to suffer from falling and sliding ice. In one accident, on 30 April 1981, part of a glacier in the Grand Combin range (Valais) swept down a mountain side killing six climbers (*The Guardian*, 4.5.81) (see also Zsigmondy 1886).

Where ice avalanches occur frequently, they should not cause many problems, for the hazards they pose can be identified and avoided. Unfortunately, there have been times when animals or people have ventured into areas of known avalanche danger with inevitable consequences. Thus, Ball (1875) has described how an ice avalanche, which was feeding one of the regenerated glaciers in the Jungfrau area, killed 300 cows. Likewise, the avalanches which frequently break away from the snout of the Le Tour glacier proved fatal in 1949 when one of them killed six walkers (Sourbier 1950; Glaister 1951; Grove 1966; Bachmann 1979; Vivian 1979) (see also Ch. 3). The rusting sign which now warns people to avoid the danger area is doubtless ignored by the more foolhardy (Plate 5). A persistent hazard also exists where villages have been unwisely sited in places exposed to ice avalanches. Randa in the Swiss Alps (Chs 6

Plate 5   Sign near Le Tour warning of glacier hazards.

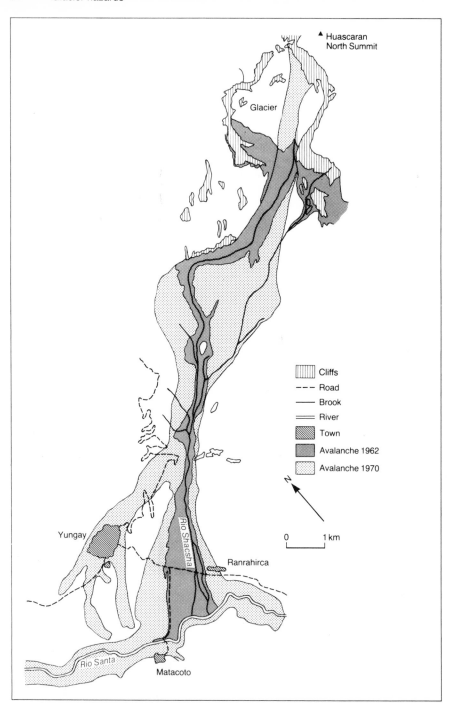

Fig 5.2   The tracks of the 1962 and 1970 Huascaràn avalanches. (After Welsch and Kinzl, 1970).

and 7) and the villages of La Gurra and La Savine in the High Tarentaise (Vivian 1979) are examples of this. In such cases, the only acceptable solution is to abandon the village and relocate it in a safer position.

The most deadly ice avalanches are those whose occurrence is unpredictable, because they are the product of factors which combine on an irregular and usually well spaced-out time-scale. The 1962 Huascaràn avalanche was of this kind, for no similar event had been recorded in the area for at least several hundred years. Moreover, the avalanche (and associated debris) penetrated no less than 16 km from its source and descended through a vertical elevation of 4,000 m. Given also the tremendous volume and speed of the moving mass, it is not surprising that it wrought great havoc and left 4,000 people dead (Table 5.1) (McDowell 1962; Rüegg 1962; Morales 1966; Lliboutry 1971, 1975; Röthlisberger 1977).

Table 5.1   The impact of the 1962 Huascaràn ice avalanche (after Morales 1966)

1. 4,000 people killed, 6 villages destroyed, 3 partly destroyed.

2. Up to 600 ha of agricultural land lost, together with many thousands of sheep, cows, pigs, goats, horses, poultry and fruit trees.

3. 10 small flour mills and 4 bridges destroyed.

Even more devastating was the 1970 Huascaràn catastrophe, for it killed between 15,000 and 20,000 people, most of whom were in the town of Yungay, which only just escaped destruction by the 1962 avalanche (Fig. 5.2). Welsch and Kinzl (1970) have described the 1970 event as the greatest glacier catastrophe in history, but this is not strictly accurate, as it involved much more than the avalanching of ice. The disaster began with a severe earthquake which caused landslides on Huascaràn. One of these brought with it great amounts of ice and thereby formed a rapidly moving mass (with speeds of 400 km/hour or greater) which was accompanied by a violent wind and was at least double the volume of the 1962 avalanche (Lliboutry 1975). These events are significant for two main reasons. First, they illustrate the problem of attempting to categorize natural events, for the 1970 disaster, unlike that of 1962, was not caused by a true avalanche, even though glacier ice was involved. Secondly, they give a measure of the severity achieved by extreme natural processes which are at least partly derived from glacial activity. As mentioned in Chapter 3, the Chamonix valley represents a classic locality for the study of glacier fluctuations and their human impact: equally, it can be maintained that during recent decades the Cordillera Blanca region of Peru has become a classic area for investigating the hazards posed by glacier *débâcles* and ice avalanches.

CHAPTER 6
GLACIER FLUCTUATIONS AND HAZARDS IN VALAIS

Nowhere has there been such an intimate encounter between glaciers and man as in the European Alps and in no other area has that encounter been so fully documented. For British geographers there is the further advantage that the Alps are one of the most accessible areas possessing well-developed glaciers. The western Alps in particular have long fascinated British travellers and scientists. On occasion, these people have made valuable observations of glacier hazards. For example, Murray (1829), Hall (1841) and Lyell (1881) all visited Martigny shortly after it was devastated by the glacier flood of 1818 and left graphic descriptions of what they found. This incident is, in fact, one of many hazardous events caused by glacier fluctuations during historic times in the Swiss canton of Valais. Because this canton has suffered a variety of glacier hazards which have been relatively well documented, it is an obvious choice for detailed study. There is also the advantage that man's responses to those hazards have ranged widely, from the naive to the sophisticated. An examination of these responses will therefore illustrate many of the approaches which have so far been tried in an effort to overcome the problems caused by glacier fluctuations. At the same time it demonstrates the frequent inadequacy of such responses and underlines the need for new ones to be developed.

VALAIS: THE PHYSICAL BACKGROUND

Valais (German: Wallis) is the third largest canton in the Swiss confederation (Fig. 6.1). It lies in the south of the country adjacent to the Italian and French borders and is wholly within the Alps. Its lowest parts are less than 400 m above sea-level and occur where the Rhône river enters Lake Geneva (Le Léman). However, the canton is on the whole very mountainous, having peaks which often rise to altitudes of over 4,000 m. The greatest elevations tend to be along the Swiss–Italian border and reach 4,634 m with the summit of Monte Rosa. Owing to the many wide altitudinal ranges within the canton, sharp peaks and ridges, steep slopes and deep valleys are common. There is also a wide variety of environments, ranging from the warm, dry climate of the Rhône valley floor to the wet and windy periglacial and glacial habitats of the high mountains.

Upstream from Martigny, the deep valley of the Rhône effectively bisects the canton. To the north of the river are the mountains of the Bernese Oberland and Aar Massif, while to the south the area is dominated by the Pennine Alps. There is also a small part of Valais which protrudes from the rest and forms a narrow band of mountainous terrain immediately west of the Rhône, between Martigny and Lake Geneva.

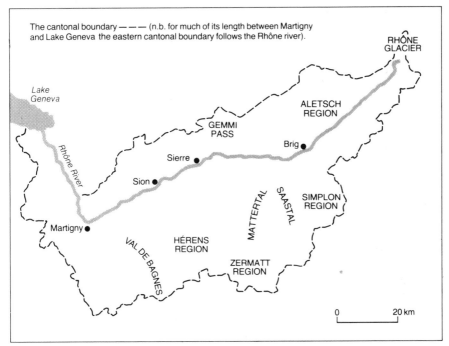

Fig 6.1 Valais canton: location map. The principal glaciers mentioned in the text are as follows:
1) Val de Bagnes: Otemma, Crête Sèche, Giétro, Durand, Boveyre, Corbassière.
2) Hérens region: Ferpècle, Mont Miné, Arolla, Tsidjiore Nouve.
3) Zermatt region + Mattertal: Gorner, Findel, Z'mutt, Grenz, Monte Rosa, Hohberg, Festi, Bies, Ried.
4) Saastal: Allalin, Schwarzberg, Gruben, Hohlaub, Trift.
5) Simplon region: Hohmatt.
6) Aletsch region: Great Aletsch, Fiesch.
7) Gemmi pass: Altels.
The position of other glaciers and localities within the canton may be found on either sheet 3 of the *Landeskarte der Schweiz* (1:200,000) or the tourist map of Valais (1:200,000) published by Kümmerly & Frey, Bern.

The Swiss Rhône valley has a rather strange course. From the Lake to Martigny it is aligned NNW–SSE. It then turns through 90°, so that between Martigny and Sierre the alignment becomes ENE-WSW. This is followed by a section which runs E–W until near Brig there is a change to a NE–SW orientation. From Lake Geneva upstream as far as Brig the Rhône valley is essentially flat floored and steep sided. In its natural state this part of the valley was badly drained and marshy, so flooding was common and disease (e.g. malaria) was widespread. During the 1860s, however, the Rhône was confined between embankments for much of its course between Lake Geneva and Brig. Additional improvements since then have further helped to reduce flooding and have also made the valley more suitable for agriculture and settlement. In a few places the relief of the valley floor is diversified by hills, which have originated either as rock falls (e.g. near Sierre) or due to the outcropping of resistant strata (e.g. at Sion). A more subdued form of relief diversity is provided by the alluvial cones which occur where tributaries debouch into the main valley. Perhaps the finest of these is at the mouth of the Illgraben, near Leuk.

Table 6.1 Increases of altitude and precipitation in the upper Rhône valley

LOCALITY	ALTITUDE (m)	ANNUAL PRECIPITATION (mm) (1901–40 average)
Brig	678	728
Reckingen	1,332	1,094
Gletsch	1,760	1,690
Furka	2,406	1,960

Source: Mariétan 1955.

Directly upstream from Brig the Rhône valley is narrower and acquires a V-shaped cross profile, which then becomes U-shaped above Fiesch. This latter section of the valley is often called *Goms* or *la vallée de Conches*, names which are derived from the Celtic *cwm* or *combe*. Throughout the length of the two sections the long profile rises more steeply than in the valley downstream from Brig and there is a parallel increase in precipitation (Table 6.1).

Valais north of the Rhône consists of two physical regions. In the west is part of the Bernese Oberland, while to the east, starting at Leuk and forming a somewhat larger area, is a section of the Aar Massif. Though both regions are mountainous, they differ in a number of important respects. First, the rocks of the Bernese Oberland are chiefly limestone and flysch, whereas in the Aar Massif crystalline strata predominate. Secondly, there are a number of peaks (Finsteraarhorn, Aletschhorn, Jungfrau, etc.) which rise to over 4,000 m in the Aar Massif section of the canton, whereas in its Oberland part the highest summit (the Wildhorn) is only 3,248 m above sea-level. Finally, glaciers are larger and much more widespread in the north-east of the canton than they are in the Oberland.

Valais, south of the Rhône, is more extensive than those parts of the canton which lie north of the river. As the southern and northern boundaries of the canton tend to follow principal watersheds, the Rhône's southern tributaries are longer and more important than their northern counterparts. Not surprisingly, they have dissected their landscape more deeply, so that the interfluves between them are pronounced geomorphological features. Indeed, these support a number of peaks which exceed 4,000 m and one (the Dom: 4,545 m) which is the highest mountain entirely within Switzerland. At their southern ends these interfluves join the main E–W running watershed which forms the Swiss–Italian border. This too has several peaks exceeding 4,000 m (Monte Rosa, Breithorn, Matterhorn, etc.). The height of this watershed and of the ridges which run northwards from it is a major reason for the widespread development of glaciers in southern Valais, though at least two other factors have also been important. One is the tendency for precipitation to increase as altitudes rise from the floor of the Rhône valley to either the interfluve summits or the heads of the southern tributary valleys (Table 6.2). The other is that Valais lies on the northern side of the main E–W watershed and therefore has more shaded slopes than its Italian counterparts. As a result, the Swiss glaciers which flow from this watershed are more impressive than those on the Italian side. That part of Valais which lies between Martigny and Lake Geneva and which protrudes from the rest is largely composed of mountainous terrain. Although precipitation is greater here than in many other parts of the canton (Table 6.3), only in the south, around the Dents du Midi (3,257 m), are altitudes just sufficient for the maintenance of small glaciers.

Because of mountainous terrain, pronounced altitudinal variations and crustal instability, Valais experiences a wide range of natural hazards. Those which stem from

Table 6.2 Increases in altitude and precipitation along the Hérens–Hérémence valley

LOCALITY	ALTITUDE (m)	ANNUAL PRECIPITATION (mm) (1901–40 average)
Sion	551	588
Hérémence	1,205	679
Grande Dixence	2,166	900

Source: Bezinge and Bonvin 1974.

Table 6.3 Precipitation at Martigny and in the area immediately west of the town

LOCALITY	ALTITUDE (m)	ANNUAL PRECIPITATION (mm) (1901–40 average)
Martigny-Ville	471	771
Châtelard	1,130	1,157
Barberine	1,822	1,640

Source: Bezinge and Bonvin 1974.

geomorphological processes include various types of mass movement, snow and ice avalanches, earthquakes, river floods, glacier outbursts and glacier fluctuations (Tufnell 1980). In addition, the canton experiences important climatic hazards, such as the föhn wind, late spring frosts and drought. Other environmental problems are the result of human activity, especially industrial and vehicle pollution. The aluminium factories at Martigny, Chippis, Steg and Visp give rise to one of the most widely discussed forms of industrial pollution within the canton. Any examination of the glacier problem in Valais must therefore be set against a background of widespread natural and man-induced hazards.

VALAISAN GLACIERS AND THEIR FLUCTUATIONS

All parts of Valais have been glaciated on several occasions in recent geological times. At present, however, only two areas within the canton are extensively glacierized. One, in north-eastern Valais, is centred on the Konkordiaplatz, a locality where several glaciers meet and where the thickest ice in the Alps (at least 800 m) has been recorded. It is from here that the Great Aletsch glacier is discharged. This is the largest of the Alpine glaciers and one of the most closely investigated. The next valley to the east contains the Fiesch glacier, which is the third largest in Valais (Table 6.4). Nearby are other important glaciers associated with the two ridges which confine the upper Lötschental.

A second, more extensive area of glaciers occurs on and near the canton's southern boundary. Here the main ice masses are associated with the important watershed along the Swiss–Italian frontier and with the ridges which run northwards from it. That part of the frontier from the Monte Moro pass to Mont Vélan has a more or less continuous ice cover, but elsewhere along the watershed glaciers are less common. Of the ridges which go northwards from this watershed, those on either side of the Mattertal support the most impressive glaciers. Since there are also large glaciers at the head of the Mattertal, the Zermatt region has a particular importance in glaciol-

Table 6.4 Dimensions of the ten principal glaciers in Valais

GLACIER	AREA (km²)	LENGTH (km)
Great Aletsch	86.76	24.7
Gorner	68.86	14.1
Fiesch	33.06	16.0
Oberaletsch	21.71	9.1
Findel	19.09	9.3
Rhône	17.38	10.2
Corbassière	17.44	9.8
Z'mutt	17.22	8.5
Otemma	16.55	8.5
Zinal	16.24	8.0

Source: Müller 1977.

Table 6.5 Altitudes of some glacier termini in the western Alps

LOCALITY	ALTITUDE (m)	
VALAIS		
Gorner	2,060	
Findel	2,320	Zermatt area
Z'mutt	2,230	
Great Aletsch	1,510	
Fiesch	1,650	North-eastern
Rhône	2,130	Valais
OTHER PARTS OF SWITZERLAND		
Upper Grindelwald	1,230	
Lower Grindelwald	1,240	
FRANCE (CHAMONIX AREA)		
Argentière	1,550	
Mer de Glace	1,480	
Bossons	1,190	

Source: Müller 1977.

ogical studies. Among the twenty-four glaciers hereabouts are three (the Gorner, Findel and Z'mutt) of the largest in Valais (Renaud 1963) (Table 6.4). The area is, however, noted for its dryness and abundant sunshine, with Zermatt having only 704 mm precipitation a year (1901–40 average) (Bezinge and Bonvin 1974). Hence, its glaciers terminate at higher altitudes than do those in many other parts of the western Alps (Table 6.5). Bezinge (1978) has pointed out that if the climate of Zermatt were the same as that of Chamonix (1934–60 precipitation average: 1,256 mm), a glacier would extend from the head of the Mattertal as far as Randa or even St Niklaus.

During recent years the history of Valaisan glaciers has been carefully examined in several important papers (Röthlisberger 1976; Schneebeli 1976; Winistorfer 1977; Aubert 1980). As expected, the story which these workers have unravelled is one of the great complexity, a point clearly demonstrated by the lists of Holocene events in

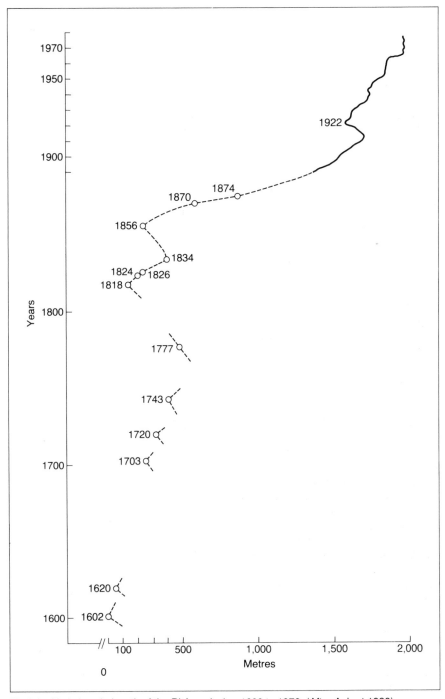

Fig 6.2 Variations in length of the Rhône glacier, 1600 to 1976. (After Aubert 1980).

the canton which have been produced by Röthlisberger (1976) and Schneebeli (1976). Even within the last 1,000 years there have been some notable changes in glacier extent and thickness. When the present millennium began, partway through the Medieval Optimum (Table 2.1. p. 7), climate was relatively warm and Valaisan glaciers were in a shrunken state. Carbon$_{14}$ dating of wood fragments has, however, shown that by the early thirteenth century the Aletsch glacier was advancing into forest. Almost 100 years later the tongue of the Allalin glacier had entered and blocked the main Saas valley, which indicates an expansion of ice greater than that of the present (Lütschg 1926, Ladurie 1967, 1972; Mercer 1975a).

The medieval advances are thought to have been followed by a respite from glacier attack which lasted between about 1350 and 1550. Thereafter, the ice returned with even greater severity. The first high point of glacier expansion in the Little Ice Age was reached during the seventeenth century, though the timing of this maximum differed throughout Valais and adjacent areas. Thus, the Chamonix glaciers were large in the early years of the century, whereas those of the Ferret and Bagnes valleys reached their maximum between 1618 and 1625. In the Hérens and Visp valleys the high point was more recent still, being from 1639 to 1660 at Mattmark (Winistorfer 1977). On the other hand, in the north-east of the canton, the Rhône glacier achieved its greatest Little Ice Age expansion in 1602 (Aubert 1980) (Fig. 6.2), at the same time as the nearby Grindelwald glaciers (Messerli et al. 1975, 1978) (Fig. 2.4, p. 18). The seventeenth-century thrust of Valaisan glaciers was followed by around 150 years when termini continued in an expanded, if slightly less advanced position. Another major thrust then occurred during the first half of the nineteenth century, in particular around 1820 and 1850. This has been well chronicled by Richter (1891) and Ladurie (1967, 1972), both of whom give information about the timing of individual glacier maxima. Directly after this high point (i.e. in the late 1850s and early 1860s), the first signs of an important and widespread retreat began to appear, even though some glaciers (e.g. the Ferpècle) persisted in an expanded state for a few years longer.

The period 1860–1960 was dominated by a retreat of Valaisan glaciers which probably constitutes one of the greatest fluctuations of their termini in historic times. Indeed, it is possible to identify only two brief periods when this retreat was interrupted. The first, during the 1890s, caused glaciers to advance slightly and this enabled many of them to build a small morainic ridge. Around 1920 there was a further advance, rather more pronounced than that of the 1890s, but still of only minor consequence. Then followed another recession, which was especially marked in the 1940s (Forel 1901; Röthlisberger et al. 1980). According to Bezinge (1978), Valaisan glaciers diminished by around 160 km^2 between 1915 and 1968. More specifically, this author has considered the details of retreat as they affected the glaciers of the Zermatt and Hérens valleys between 1930 and 1970 (Bezinge 1971).

In 1964–65 the first signs appeared that the marked retreat of the previous 100 years might be coming to an end. Since then, in the eleven years to 1974–75, there has been only one occasion (1970–71) when conditions have been highly unfavourable for Swiss glaciers (Table 6.6) (Kasser and Aellen 1976). During the last few years, some remarkable glacier advances have occurred in the Valaisan Alps and details of these have even reached the popular press. For example, on 11 September 1980 the paper *La Suisse* contained a headline which read 'Glacier fou en Valais'. It was referring to the Findel glacier near Zermatt which had advanced 70 m over the previous eighteen months. Despite the fairly numerous thrusts of Valaisan glaciers in recent years, it is difficult to assess the significance of current trends. They may represent only a temporary interruption in a long period of recession or they could signify the beginning of a protracted climatic deterioration and expansion of glaciers.

Table 6.6 Glacier variations in the Swiss Alps, 1964–5 to 1974–5 (after Kasser and Aellen 1976)

YEAR	% GLACIERS OBSERVED		
	Advancing	Stationary	Retreating
1964–5	24.4	11.1	64.5
1965–6	37.3	3.3	59.4
1966–7	23.0	3.0	74.0
1967–8	35.7	6.1	58.2
1968–9	27.2	4.8	68.0
1969–70	31.6	6.1	62.3
1970–1	15.8	4.6	79.6
1971–2	39.0	7.0	54.0
1972–3	25.3	8.4	66.3
1973–4	39.5	18.4	42.1
1974–5	52.3	10.3	37.4

Although every Valaisan glacier has broadly followed the pattern just outlined, the *precise* timings and extent of fluctuations have often varied with the individual. Thus, Lütschg (1916) pointed out differences in the fluctuations of the Allalin and nearby Schwarzberg glaciers. Likewise, Roethlisberger and Schneebeli (1979) have noted that the Crête Sèche retreated more than 3 km between 1859 and 1965, whereas a short distance away the tongue of the Giétro glacier shrank by only 300 m over the same period because it was at a greater altitude (Fig. 6.3).

THE PROBLEMS CAUSED BY VALAISAN GLACIERS

Given the location of the main ice masses within Valais, it is evident that glacier hazards must have traditionally been concentrated in two principal areas. One of these lies on or near the canton's southern boundary and includes areas such as the Zermatt region and the Val de Bagnes. The other is situated in the north-east of the canton and is centred around the Great Aletsch glacier. However, some hazards have managed to extend their influence well beyond these ice-covered regions. Glacier floods in particular have often spread their destruction down into the main Rhône valley.

Problems have tended to be most acute when the climate was cooler and Valaisan glaciers were in an enlarged state. On the other hand, some hazards could only have arisen due to climatic improvement and glacier retreat. The variety and frequency of glacier hazards experienced within the canton have been appreciable and have added to the region's already considerable environmental problems (Tufnell 1980).

The impact of glacier fluctuations

On settlement

Among those who observed at first hand the damage caused by the expansion of Valaisan glaciers were a number of British scientists. For example, in September 1857 Charles Lyell described how he saw 'beams of wooden chalets and roofing tiles' in the terminal moraine of the Gorner glacier (Lyell 1881). During August of the following year John Tyndall visited the same locality and was told 'that within the last sixty

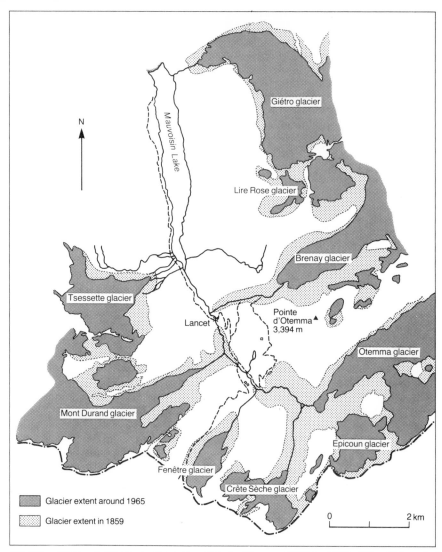

N

Giétro glacier

Mauvoisin Lake

Lire Rose glacier

Brenay glacier

Tsessette glacier

Lancet

Pointe d'Otemma ▲ 3,394 m

Otemma glacier

Mont Durand glacier

Épicoun glacier

Fenêtre glacier

Crête Sèche glacier

▓ Glacier extent around 1965

░ Glacier extent in 1859

0   2 km

Fig 6.3 Glacier shrinkage in the upper Val de Bagnes, 1859 to 1965. (After Schneebeli, 1976).

years forty-four chalets had been overturned by the glacier' (Tyndall 1911). Also in the middle of the last century, the nearby hamlet of Findeln was being threatened by the close approach of the Findel glacier (Bachmann 1979). Likewise, it is known that the stream which flows from the Z'mutt glacier has often brought down household and other items, and it has long been said that the remains of a small settlement lie buried beneath the ice (Lehner, no date). Recently, the existence of such a settlement was convincingly demonstrated by F. Röthlisberger (1974, 1976), who used the following data to support his arguments: (a) the name of the village (Tiefenmatten) is known; (b) there is a glacier of the same name; (c) a village has traditionally been said to exist at the foot of the Hohwäng and Schönbüel mountains; (d) farm implements have been retrieved from the Z'mutt glacier; (e) fragments of tree trunks have been discovered at the snout of the Z'mutt glacier; (f) a forest has been found at a

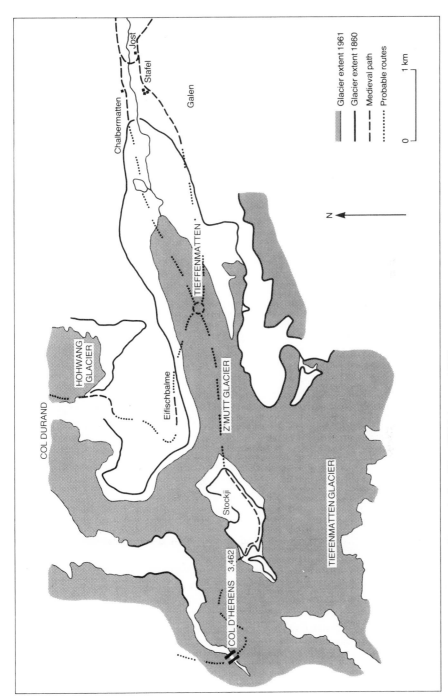

Fig 6.4 Tiefenmatten and the Z'mutt glacier. (After Röthlisberger, 1976).

depth of 11 m below the ground moraine of the Z'mutt glacier; and (g) four paths disappear under the Z'mutt glacier moraines and these make it possible to fix the exact location of Tiefenmatten (Fig. 6.4). They show the village to have been at the crossroads of routes from the glacier passes of the Col d'Hérens, the Col Durand and the Theodul pass. It is believed that Tiefenmatten was inhabited during the Middle Ages and was obviously destroyed by a glacier advance much earlier than that witnessed by Lyell (1881) and Tyndall (1911).

At about the time the Gorner glacier was causing problems near Zermatt, the Great Aletsch was destroying barns as it reached its 1849 maximum (Bérard 1976). Nearby, an advance of the Fiesch glacier overran the chapel of Titer (Bachmann 1979), while in southern Valais the common tongue of the Ferpècle and Mont Miné glaciers was also causing problems. Even as late as 1868, this tongue was only a few metres from buildings near Salay (F. Röthlisberger 1974, 1976).

On agriculture and woodland

In addition to noting the destruction of chalets by the Gorner glacier, Tyndall (1911) remarked on the meadows which were 'partly shrivelled up by its irresistible advance'. Similarly, Lyell (1881) observed that the moraines of the Gorner and Findel glaciers contained 'fresh green turf of meadows rolled up and mixed confusedly with mud and stones'. He also saw places where the Gorner glacier 'had penetrated some eighty feet last year', though elsewhere 'it had moved forward much less'. The nearby Z'mutt glacier must have destroyed pastureland as well, for the name of the lost settlement of Tiefenmatten means 'low' or 'valley bottom meadows'. However, none of the Zermatt glaciers began invading agricultural land until after 1400 and all had ceased to do so by the last quarter of the nineteenth century (F. Röthlisberger 1974, 1976).

Similar events occurred in other parts of Valais. For example, Mathews (1926), who visited the Val de Bagnes in 1856, saw the Otemma and Durand glaciers 'ploughing up . . . pasture'. Likewise, Forel (1888) was told that meadows had been overrun during the 1817–18 advances of the Ferpècle/Mont Miné glacier. As in the Zermatt valley, this area had been farmed during medieval times: it first experienced glacier incursions during the fifteenth century and continued to suffer from them until the later decades of the nineteenth century (Buhrer 1904; F. Röthlisberger 1974, 1976). Equally interesting is a report that in 1653 the Aletsch glacier was threatening fields not far from Naters. Happily, on this occasion a retreat set in before the ice became too troublesome (Ladurie 1967, 1972). On the other hand, there is reference in an old manuscript to an apple tree which used to grow on a spot that was beneath the Aletsch glacier at the beginning of the present century. Also at this time, the ruins of a grain store were visible, situated in an area devoid of vegetation and covered with stones (Buhrer 1904).

Valaisan farmers also suffered from the inclement weather which is typically associated with periods of glacier advance. It has been said that during the bad years of the Little Ice Age there was frost every month at Zermatt. The quality of pastureland therefore deteriorated and the harvests became very poor. Due to the resultant starvation, many people left the area (Lehner, no date). Conditions were equally bad in the neighbouring Saastal. There too harvests were often poor and during the first half of the seventeenth century several years could pass without the corn being able to ripen. In addition, trees at high altitudes failed to turn completely green (Bérard 1976; Ruppen, Imseng and Imseng 1979).

Trees, like pastureland, can be overrun by an advancing glacier. This has been a fairly frequent and long-standing occurrence in Valais, as demonstrated by the following:

1. There have been quite a few discoveries of tree fragments in the morainic debris left by former glacier advances. Dating of these fragments has shown that trees were being destroyed by glacier thrusts even before historic times (Bezinge and Vivian 1976; Röthlisberger 1976; Roethlisberger and Schneebeli 1979; Röthlisberger *et al* 1980).

2. There have been observations of glaciers actually destroying trees. In 1857, Lyell (1881) found eight larches in the moraine of the Gorner glacier which had 'their boughs and trunks protruding in horizontal and oblique directions'. He also described the nearby Findel glacier as 'felling fir trees'. Likewise, a memoir published by Collomb in 1857 tells how the Z'mutt glacier was ravaging an ancient forest and overturning many of its trees. Some years previously, in 1849, both the Aletsch and Fiesch glaciers had reached a maximum and in doing so had overrun trees. Those destroyed by the Fiesch glacier were said to be 200–300 years old. Similarly, in 1816, the Trient glacier was invading an area of forest. A pre-nineteenth-century advance is mentioned in an act which tells of woodland in the Val de Bagnes that became covered by a glacier (perhaps the Boveyre or Corbassière). Earlier still is a record of forest destruction by the Aletsch glacier: this probably occurred at the beginning of the thirteenth century and shows that during the last millennium some invasions of forest by Valaisan glaciers have taken place outside of the Little Ice Age (Buhrer 1904; Lütschg 1926: Ladurie 1967, 1972; Bérard 1976).

On water supply

As many parts of Valais receive only small amounts of precipitation, there has long been a need to search for water. Man has found that in this quest glaciers have been both helpful and unreliable. They have been helpful in providing important quantities of meltwater for crop irrigation and, more recently, for hydroelectricity developments. On the other hand, the reliability of this supply has been undermined by repeated fluctuations in the extent and thickness of glaciers and in the meltwater they have produced.

Even today there are many localities which preserve evidence of Valais' extensive system of irrigation channels known as *les bisses*. Of more than 200 such channels which occur in the canton, the majority whose period of construction is known date from the fourteenth and fifteenth centuries. This is because water was scarce at that time, for glaciers were in a shrunken state and were making a correspondingly reduced contribution to stream flow. By contrast, during the Little Ice Age, when glaciers were larger, virtually no *bisses* were constructed (Bérard 1976). Indeed, some were actually overrun by the advancing glaciers. This was the case in the Mattertal where expansion of the Ried glacier interfered with *bisses* serving Grächen, St Niklaus and Herbriggen (Mariétan 1952). Hardships must have ensued, for this is the driest part of Switzerland: Grächen has an annual precipitation of only 56 cm, while nearby Staldenried gets as little as 53 cm (Gutersohn 1961). Another interesting case is that of the Oberriederin, an irrigation channel which was overrun by the Aletsch glacier. This example shows that some irrigation channels were operating before the main period of *bisse* construction in the fourteenth and fifteenth centuries, and that glacier thrusts which pre-dated those of the Little Ice Age also caused problems for the people of Valais – it seems that glacier expansion had already made the Oberriederin unusable by the late twelfth/early thirteenth centuries (Ladurie 1967, 1972).

During more modern times the *bisse* system has fallen into decline, but the need for meltwater remains as great as ever. This is chiefly because important hydroelectric schemes have been developed in Valais. The largest of these is the Grande Dixence scheme, which takes 380 million m^3 of water each year from the Mattertal and the Val d'Hérens. At present, half of the scheme's catchment area is glaciated.

On communications and trade

Because Valais is a mountain canton, communications and trade have always proved difficult. The Rhône valley is still the only good internal route, as well as the only easy link with the outside world. Even this was not so before the 1860s when the first significant efforts were made to confine the Rhône river between embankments and reduce the marshy nature of the flat valley floor. Given this situation, Valaisans traditionally found it necessary to use a number of mountain passes in order to communicate and trade among themselves and with their neighbours. The difficulties encountered on some of these passes have varied as glaciers waxed and waned.

Perhaps the best-known illustration of this relates to the Col d'Hérens, a high-level pass joining the heads of the Mattertal and the Val d'Hérens. In medieval times nine people from Zermatt walked annually over this pass and down the Val d'Hérens to the important ecclesiastical centre of Sion. Apparently it was much quicker to go this way than to take the route down the Matter–Visp and Rhône valleys. The purpose of their journey was to pray in Sion for the protection of their fellow villagers from hazards. Eventually, however, these people were forced to ask that their prayers be said nearer home because glacier expansion was making the Col d'Hérens route very dangerous. This request was granted in 1666 when the bishop of Sion allowed them to use the church at nearby Täsch for their purpose (Buhrer 1904; Harriss 1971; F. Röthlisberger 1974, 1976; Lüthi 1978).

Like many other stories, this emphasizes the rather well-known fact that in Valais, as elsewhere in the Alps, communications were affected by the glacier advances of the Little Ice Age. However, it is less widely appreciated that some routes within the canton have actually become more difficult owing to glacier retreat. An example is the route across the Ferpècle glacier from Bricola to Mont Miné. When Forbes visited the area in 1842 the glacier was in an enlarged state, so it was quite easy for sheep to be driven across it in search of pasture. Today the journey would be virtually impossible because glacier shrinkage has uncovered steep slopes of rock and moraine. Climatic improvement has also brought about an opening of crevasses which has increased the hazards along some routes (Forbes 1900; F. Röthlisberger 1974).

While the Col d'Hérens story illustrates the religious and social function of mountain passes, it says nothing of their value as trade routes. Indeed, this pass was always less important for commerce than were its neighbours which straddle the Swiss–Italian border. These include the Antrona, Monte Moro, Theodul and Collon passes. During their heyday they witnessed the frequent movement of goods between the northern and southern valleys of the Pennine divide. Cereals, rice, fruit, cheese and wine from the warmer Italian valleys were sent northwards over these passes in return for the cattle, sheep, leather goods, wool cloth and salt of Valais. Interdependence of trade also brought about periods when the two areas were politically and ecclesiastically united and their populations intermingled. However, by the fifteenth century there were signs of glaciers encroaching on to previously ice-free routes. The associated climatic deterioration influenced the region's cereal and pastoral economy, while the advancing glaciers made the transfer of produce increasingly difficult. A treaty dating from 1440 mentions that ice was beginning to affect the Monte Moro area, and by 1528 the Theodul pass was occupied by a large glacier, whereas previously it had been ice-free. Such events had the effect of separating what had once been interdependent communities. During the Little Ice Age there were at times minor improvements in the situation, which encouraged attempts to reopen the passes, but these met with only temporary success. This was the case, for example, with the Monte Moro pass which was briefly reopened on several occasions during the eighteenth century, but which did not get a more lasting climatic reprieve until after the middle of the nineteenth century. By then, however, other developments had begun which were permanently to reduce the importance of high-level glacier passes in the Zermatt region. Among the earliest were the improvements ordered by Napoleon to the Simplon and St Bernard passes (Buhrer 1904; Harriss 1970, 1971, 1972; F. Röthlisberger 1974; Lüthi 1978; Ruppen, Imseng and Imseng 1979).

Outside the Zermatt region there are other high-level passes whose fortunes have been affected by the oscillations of Valaisan glaciers. One of these provided a route between Liddes in the Val d'Entremont and the adjacent Val de Bagnes. However, this eventually became impracticable due to the expansion of a glacier (possibly the Boveyre or the Corbassière). A similar fate appears to have befallen the Col de Fenêtre which up to around 1600 was a frequently used route between the Val de Bagnes and Aosta (Buhrer 1904; Agassiz 1967; Bérard 1976). Likewise in northeastern Valais the Wetterlücke provided a route between the Lötschen and Lauterbrunnen valleys before it was abandoned due to advances of the Breithorn glacier. Again, decline of the Lötschen pass, which joined the Gasterental and the Lötschental, is at least partly attributable to glacier encroachment: however, it was also due to improvements of the route over the nearby Gemmi pass (Ball 1875; Coolidge 1908; Agassiz 1967). This example illustrates well the need for caution when trying to assess the effects of glacier fluctuations on the use of mountain passes in Valais. The point has been forcibly made by F. Röthlisberger (1974), who prefaced his study of the Col d'Hérens with a list of non-glacial factors which might influence the use of mountain passes. Failure to appreciate this point has inevitably led to mistaken interpretations. There is, for example, a story which claims that during medieval times, when glaciers were small, Protestants from eastern Valais used to journey over the Great Aletsch glacier and Mönchjoch to Grindelwald. However, it has been found that this story is incorrect and arose because some people, who were natives of Valais, had their children baptized at Grindelwald. In fact, they did so merely because they were living there at the time (Forbes 1900).

The impact of glacier outbursts

The area of Valais with the worst history of glacier outbursts is undoubtedly the Val de Bagnes and the town of Martigny. As early as the sixth century the bishop's seat was moved to Sion because of the way these outbursts were affecting Martigny. The main cause of the problem was expansion of the Giétro glacier, which occupies a tributary in the upper Val de Bagnes. Over recent centuries advances by this glacier have led to several destructive floods. The earliest of these overwhelmed Martigny and swept away numerous bridges. Murray (1829), who was quoting a manuscript in the St Bernard hospice, and Lütschg (1926) say this flood happened in 1469, but Muret (1901), Schneebeli (1976) and Bachmann (1979) claim it was 1549. Another year, 1459, has been given for a flood which also ravaged Martigny and destroyed many bridges. However, this is supposed to have come down the Val d'Entremont, which would exclude the Giétro glacier as its source (Mariétan 1970). Significantly, the date 7 August was mentioned by all these authors, which at least suggests they were referring to the same event. By contrast, there appear to be no doubts about the timing of a second outburst, for all agree that this took place in 1595. It destroyed around 500 buildings and caused nearly 150 deaths, half of which were in Martigny. A similar, though apparently less disastrous outburst occurred in 1640, but details of this are rather scarce. However, none of the earlier floods has gained the notoriety achieved by that of 1818. This devastated the Val de Bagnes and Martigny, killing around 50 people and many animals. It destroyed 359 buildings, numerous sections of road and many bridges, and did considerable damage to the harvest and to orchards (Pictet 1819; Murray 1829; Richter 1891; Forbes 1900; Muret 1901; Rabot 1905; Lütschg 1926; Mariétan 1959, 1970; Ladurie 1967, 1972; Schneebeli 1976; Bachmann 1979; Vivian 1979). Great amounts of erosion were accomplished, as noted by Hall (1841) and Lyell (1881), both of whom made on-site observations of the effects of the catastrophe. Hall, for example, tells how he went into the church at Martigny and found that: 'The pulpit just peeped above the mass of rubbish, but the altar was . . . quite buried under the mud.' He also mentioned that:'In every house . . . there lay a stratum of alluvial matter several feet in thickness.'

Other outbursts in the Val de Bagnes were due not to advances of the Giétro glacier, but to retreat of the nearby Crête Sèche and Otemma glaciers. These outbursts arose because the two glaciers, which were formerly confluent in their down-valley sections, divided and withdrew at different rates. This meant that the ice and moraine of the more slowly retreating Otemma glacier impounded meltwater from the Crête Sèche. On several occasions in the 1890s this water was evacuated violently and there was the inevitable flooding downvalley. Chalets and bridges were destroyed, fields were covered with debris, a new channel was cut by the Drance at Lourtier and great amounts of sediment were poured into the Rhône (Mercanton 1899, 1928; Mariétan 1927a; Vivian 1974).

Likewise, separation of the formerly confluent Ferpècle and Mont Miné glaciers has produced floods in the Val d' Hérens. These occurred in 1943 and 1952 and were in August on both occasions. They were due to the rupture of meltwater pockets and caused important amounts of damage, but no loss of life (Walser 1952; Martin-Chavannes 1953).

Similar, though more persistent glacier outbursts have been observed since the seventeenth century in the nearby Mattertal. Their source has been the Gornersee, a lake which occupies a depression formed by the confluence of the Gorner and Grenz glaciers. As the extent of these glaciers has fluctuated, so the dimensions and shape of the lake have varied. Its fullest development has occurred when the glaciers have been in retreat, though were this process to go too far, the depression and its lake would disappear. The Gornersee outbursts are part of an annual pattern which usually starts in May at the beginning of the spring melt season. Water from the Gorner, Grenz and Monte Rosa glaciers begins flowing into the lake at this time. Eventually, when the lake is full or nearly so, there is a violent evacuation of its waters. This takes place between late June and early September. Regularity of the pattern is such that very few observations have been made of two outbursts in one summer or of a year with no outburst. On the other hand, the *severity* of outbursts varies quite markedly in response to prevailing environmental conditions. Obviously, it has been the larger outbursts, such as that of 1944, which have caused the greatest erosion and the worst damage to the chalets, bridges, fields and trees of the Mattertal. This valley has also suffered, though to a lesser extent, from *débâcles* of the Hohberg and Festi glaciers. However, these have been more irregular than the Gornersee floods and have some-times occurred during winter (Bezinge, Perreten and Schafer 1973; Vivian 1974; Bezinge 1978).

At Stalden the Mattertal is joined by the Saastal: this too has had its share of outbursts, which have mostly been caused by fluctuations of the Allalin glacier. During times of cooler climate, this glacier was obviously in an enlarged state and therefore able to emerge from its side valley into the main Saastal. As a result, it has on occasion blocked the Saaser Vispa river causing the formation of a lake known as the Mattmarksee. Rupture of the glacier/moraine dam has led to sudden evacuations of this lake and flooding downvalley. One of the earliest known outbursts was in 1589, and it was followed by a series of damaging events which persisted throughout the Little Ice Age. No less than thirty outbursts of the Mattmarksee have been recorded with typical results – chalets, bridges and trees destroyed; fields not only inundated, but also subjected to both erosion and deposition. Over the last 100 or so years, glacier shrinkage and engineering works have removed the danger of lake formation and outbursts in this area (Lütschg 1926; Mariétan 1965; Ladurie 1967, 1972; Ruppen, Imseng and Imseng 1979).

Another cause of *débâcles* in the Saastal has been the Gruben glacier. This occurs in an area of low precipitation, so there is often little snow to hinder the penetration of winter cold into the glacier. As a result, cracks in the ice become firmly sealed. During the meltwater season an ice-dammed lake can therefore develop at the side of the glacier and only if a long period of very warm weather sets in will the lake burst through a thinning ice barrier. When this happened in 1957, 1968 and 1970, damage was done to buildings and fields at Saas Balen and much assorted debris was swept away (H. Röthlisberger 1974; Ruppen, Imseng and Imseng 1979).

The Allalin situation becomes 'reversed' when a glacier occupies the main valley and impounds a lake in one of its ice-free tributaries. A well-known example of this from Valais is the damming of the Märjelensee by the Aletsch glacier. Throughout its history this lake has experienced repeated changes in water-level which have often taken place rapidly. Thus, in 1858 T. G. Bonney (1887) saw the lake full one day, but empty the next, while in 1873 there was an outflow of 10 million m³ in only eight hours. Such outbursts have, like those of the Gornersee, usually occurred between June and September. They resulted from water draining away over, through or beneath the Aletsch glacier or escaping in the opposite direction via a low col into the Fiesch valley. The inundations they caused have affected the flat-floored Rhône valley, sometimes as far downriver as Lake Geneva. They have also achieved considerable erosion, as in July 1913, when 86,000 tons of alluvium were swept away in just a few hours (Preller 1896a; Collet 1926; Aubert 1980).

The impact of glacier avalanches

Glacier avalanches frequently occur in Valais, but only a few have proved destructive. In the Mattertal the village of Randa has long been exposed to falls from the Bies glacier which rests on the eastern flanks of the Weisshorn. If the weather is clear, the terminus of this glacier can easily be seen from the road between Herbriggen and Randa as it hangs threateningly on a steep slope overlooking the valley. At times, sections of this glacier have broken away and avalanched towards Randa with typical results – the damage or destruction of chalets and trees by the ice and its associated wind; interference with communications in the valley; blocking of the Matter Vispa river and the flooding of areas directly upvalley of the ice barrier. On one occasion (1636) there was also considerable loss of life (Table 6.7). Recently, an avalanche occurred in February 1980 and, although smaller than some of its predecessors, trains of the Visp–Zermatt line were still disappearing from view as they passed through an artificial cutting in its ice/debris cone at the end of April (Plate 6).

Despite a troubled history, Randa is not the place which has suffered the most disastrous ice avalanche in Valais. That unenviable distinction belongs to Mattmark

Table 6.7 Avalanche disasters at Randa

DATE	NATURE OF AVALANCHE	EFFECTS OF AVALANCHE	DATA SOURCES
1636	Glacier avalanche	36 people killed; village extensively damaged. People thought the entire glacier had fallen into the valley	Ball 1878; Bonney 1912
1720	?	12 people killed	Fraser 1966
1736 (or 1730 or 1737)	Glacier avalanche	140 buildings destroyed	Richter 1891; Mariétan 1965
1786	Glacier avalanche	?	Richter 1891
1819	Avalanche (estimated volume 12.4×10^6 m^3) started as falling ice, but became pulverized on its journey downhill	Avalanche fell to one side of village, but associated wind caused severe and widespread damage to buildings. Roofs and beams were in some cases blown over distances of 2 km. Only 2 people killed. It was proposed that village be moved to new site, but this has not happened. Large trees uprooted and thrown about. Much debris scattered over the area. Avalanche blocked the Matter Vispa river, but a cutting was made which allowed the water to escape	Tscheinen 1860; Ball 1878; Bonney 1912; Mariétan 1965; Fraser 1966; Agassiz 1967
1848	?	Matter Vispa blocked for 5 days, but as it was winter, river discharge was low and the water eventually drained away without doing much damage	Richter 1891
1865	2 glacier avalanches, one towards end of January, another in mid February. In both cases the descending ice was transformed into an airborne-powder avalanche	?	Coaz 1881
1980	Glacier avalanche	Avalanche blocked the Matter Vispa river and the Zermatt–Visp railway line. Its associated wind damaged chalets. A lake formed behind the ice barrier, but was successfully drained, partly by pumping and partly by cutting a trench up to 20 m deep. Even the oldest inhabitants of Randa could not remember so large an avalanche cone	*Nouvelliste et Feuille d'Avis du Valais*, 7 and 8 February 1980

Plate 6 Avalanche/debris cone of the Bies glacier, April 1980. The terminus of the glacier can be seen at the head of the cliffs.

in the Saastal. On 30 August 1965 this area was struck by a catastrophe in which eighty-eight people died and many buildings were destroyed. Again, the culprit was the Allalin glacier. Ironically, the retreat of this glacier from its advanced Little Ice Age positions has merely led to one danger being replaced by another. No longer does the Allalin emerge from its side valley to block the Sasser Vispa and create the Mattmarksee: instead, contraction upvalley has led to its tongue resting on a steep rocky slope in the same threatening manner as the terminus of the Bies glacier. For some years prior to the 1965 disaster the Allalin had been acting in a rather unusual way, since its terminus had been experiencing a mixture of advances and retreats, while most other glaciers were undergoing a fairly consistent shrinkage. In addition, just before the disaster the glacier's rate of movement increased to the exceptionally high figure of almost 4 m/day. The reasons for this abnormal behaviour were partly topographical and partly climatic. Of great importance must have been the steep, rocky nature of the topography underlying the glacier tongue, for it meant there was little adherence of ice to the valley floor. This influence would continue to have an effect whenever the glacier tongue rests on a steep, rocky slope. Perhaps the most significant climatic influences are precipitation patterns. Thus, it is known that advances of the Allalin correspond to increased winter precipitation, whereas retreats correlate with low precipitation amounts. The latter were especially pronounced between 1935 and 1955, while an increase of winter precipitation characterized the ten years before the catastrophe and must therefore have helped to bring it about. Also important was the wet, warm weather in the weeks before the avalanche, since this heated up the rocky bed and lubricated its contact with the glacier (Vivian 1966).

There were two main reasons why the avalanche proved so disastrous. One was the existence of buildings downslope from the glacier. These were associated with the construction of a dam, the work on which had begun in 1960. As the avalanche descended towards this complex, the preceding air blast destroyed the workmen's wooden huts. These were then buried under a layer of ice up to 20 m thick. The other factor responsible for the severity of the disaster was that the avalanche occurred when workmen were changing shifts and were therefore at the site in twice their usual number (Vivian 1966). According to Mariétan (1965), there are no reports of a similar avalanche in the past. This might be due to the glacier tongue being either longer or shorter than the optimum length for avalanching. Equally, it might be that avalanches have actually occurred, but went unrecorded due to the remoteness of the valley and its sparse population.

Immediately east of the Saastal is the Simplon region, which also has a history of ice avalanche disasters. Perhaps the earliest was in 1597 when an avalanche from the Hohmatt glacier destroyed the village of Eggen (Gutersohn 1961). More recently, in 1901, an area of weathered rock on the Fletschhorn collapsed, bringing with it two-thirds of a hanging glacier. The descending mass swept up a large amount of morainic debris. Its eventual volume, as it crashed into the valley near Eggen, was estimated at between 4 and 5 million m³. More than 80 ha of forest, fields and pastureland were covered with a layer of ice, snow and debris which in some places was over 20 m thick. The disaster killed 2 people and many farm animals; it demolished 20 or so buildings and much hay was lost. Once again, destruction was caused not only by the avalanche, but also by the associated pressure wave (e.g. the latter damaged woodland) (Muret 1901; Schardt 1902).

There have also been major ice avalanches near the summit of the Gemmi pass, on the northern borders of Valais. One of these, in August 1782, killed 4 people and 90 cattle. Another, on 11 September 1895, killed 6 people and about 150 cattle, destroyed several chalets and ruined 2 km² of Alpine pasture. It also flattened an extensive area of woodland, which was growing well downslope of the avalanche breakaway zone. Having plunged through a vertical depth of 1,400 m down the north-western face of the Altels mountain, the avalanche travelled 400 m uphill to the top of a ridge on the slopes opposite, before rebounding towards the valley floor. It covered a distance of about 5 km in no more than a minute, which indicates the considerable velocities involved. An estimated 4 million m³ of ice and debris was moved in this way and on coming to rest it formed a layer 2 m thick and around 2 km² in extent. Fortunately, none of this blocked the stream draining the valley, so no lake formed and there was no danger from flooding. The associated wind proved very destructive and scattered people, cattle and the remains of chalets over a wide area. Unlike the Randa avalanches, which have tended to be in winter, those on the Altels were late summer/early autumn phenomena. That of 1895 originated through the opening of transverse crevasses during the preceding months, which were hot and dry. It was further encouraged by the warm föhn wind which blew in the hours before the disaster and which must have increased the rate of ice melting (Preller 1896b).

CHAPTER 7
RESPONSES TO GLACIER HAZARDS IN VALAIS

Previous chapters have examined the nature of glacier fluctuations and their effects on man. It therefore remains to consider how man has responded to such hazards. Once more, it is appropriate to focus attention on Valais, since there have been varied reactions to the glacier problem within the canton. However, as elsewhere, those reactions have frequently been less sophisticated than man's response to certain other environmental hazards (e.g. floods and earthquakes). This is largely because glacier hazards were often at their most troublesome prior to the modern scientific era and also because they have had a somewhat limited distribution. As a result, man has been lulled into a complacency which makes him ill-prepared to cope with a possible glacier advance equal to or exceeding the maxima of the Little Ice Age. The present chapter therefore discusses not only the merits but also the shortcomings of man's attempts to counteract the hazards caused by glacier fluctuations. Despite these shortcomings, there is one person who may be regarded as having contributed significantly to alleviating the problem in so far as it has affected Valais. That person is the engineer Ignace Venetz (1788–1859) who shares with Agassiz and Charpentier the further distinction of having formulated early ideas about the previous extent of glaciers (Mariétan 1959). An appreciation of Venetz's work provides a useful starting-point for anyone wishing to develop new methods of protecting man from glacier hazards.

Panic, prayers and processions

The oldest and most common reaction to glacier hazards must have been fear. In an effort to allay this, man has often invoked religious sentiments. One of the earliest known examples from Valais arose due to a pronounced thrust of the Aletsch glacier in the mid seventeenth century. As the ice was threatening to overrun fields close to the village of Naters, the local inhabitants sought the aid of the Jesuits. The two who were sent preached to the villagers and afterwards accompanied them in a procession to the glacier. On reaching the terminus they performed various rituals in the hope of staying its advance. Fortunately, their efforts were successful (Lütschg 1926; Ladurie 1967, 1972).

This story is typical of many from different parts of the Alps. There were, for example, similar rituals performed in an attempt to halt the advancing glaciers of the Chamonix valley. Among the best known are those which involved the bishop of Geneva, Charles de Sales, and his successor, Jean d'Arenthon. The fact that these people had to make several visits to the glaciers during about fifty years of the seventeenth century is proof that at best their endeavours met with only limited success (Grove 1966; Ladurie 1967, 1972).

In some areas, religious processions to menacing glaciers became frequent, rather than isolated occurrences. Thus, when the expanding Ried glacier overran parts of a nearby irrigation system, people from surrounding villages undertook to celebrate the feast of St Jodern on 4 September each year. They built a sanctuary close to the glacier and went there in annual procession to say mass and to hear a sermon. Although the Ried glacier has shrunk considerably since this ritual was initiated, the feast day is still celebrated 'in a spirit of gratitude' (Mariétan 1952).

Often in the past, the misery caused by a glacier disaster has been compounded by the wretched belief that it was all somehow due to the sins of the people. Thus, in 1680, following a *débâcle* of the Allalin glacier, people vowed to abstain from dancing, feasting and gambling for forty years, because they thought they had angered God. It was also pathetically claimed that 'misfortune makes us better people, misfortune leads us to Heaven'. A number of religious festivals celebrated in the Saas valley had their origins in these vows. Almost a century later, the response to glacier hazards was essentially the same for, in 1774, when the Mattmark lake became threatening, all that the people did was to ask for public prayers in the hope of obtaining divine mercy (Lütschg 1926; Ladurie 1967, 1972; Ruppen, Imseng and Imseng 1979).

The supposed link between glacier disasters and human sins was also mentioned in a sermon preached at Geneva twelve days after the 1818 *débâcle* of the Giétro glacier. Much of this sermon was a veritable tirade of chastisements and only near the end did it adopt a more practical tone and advise those unaffected by the disaster to help the less fortunate. Interestingly, the printed version of the sermon was prefaced by the words 'Imprimé au bénéfice des victimes de ce malheur'. However, it is not clear whether the benefit intended was spiritual or material (Moulinié 1820). Indeed, prior to the nineteenth-century work of Venetz there appear to have been few practical responses to glacier hazards in Valais. The population was therefore largely unprotected and naturally looked to its religious faith to help it overcome the impact of a disaster. At times, this faith must have provided a considerable psychological boost, especially when a religious act, such as exorcism, appeared to make a glacier retreat. It is equally obvious, however, that many religious acts at glacier termini failed to produce the desired effects. Thus, their value when they were performed may well have been less than it is today, for modern scientists can use written records of such acts to help them understand glacier behaviour.

Reducing the problem

As scientific reasoning became more widespread, religious faith ceased to be the prime response to glacier hazards in Valais. Nevertheless, it still persists as one of the available responses, though its influence has long been waning. To some extent its survival must have been helped by the failures of the scientific–practical approach. No doubt, there were occasions when these failures were quickly seized upon by clergy as proof of the inadequacies of scientific reasoning. One such occasion was Moulinié's sermon on the Giétro tragedy which compares the weakness of man's attempt to prevent the *débâcle* with the might of the Lord (Moulinié 1820). Yet, when examined carefully and dispassionately, that attempt was at the very least an honourable failure, especially as it represents one of the first significant examples of how to reduce the severity of glacier hazards.

For some years prior to the tragedy an advancing Giétro glacier was pushing ice and snow over a high cliff into the Val de Bagnes, so that a regenerated glacier of conical shape began accumulating in the valley bottom. Initially, the Drance river was able to find a way through this mass, but as the ice accumulated further and consolidated, the river became increasingly obstructed until, in April 1818, it was noticed that a lake had started to form. The danger in this situation was eventually realized and of the schemes devised to prevent an outburst of lake water, that proposed by Venetz was adopted. It was based on the idea that a tunnel cut through the ice dam would stop the lake from rising above a certain height. The tunnel itself had to slope downvalley in order to carry away the excess water and, on being completed, its upper end had to be a little above what was then the surface of the lake. Eventually, as the lake filled, its waters would reach the tunnel entrance and so make their escape. It was further hoped that these waters would gradually lower the tunnel floor and that this would help reduce lake level. Excavation of the tunnel began on 13 May and took until 13 June by which time the lake's dimensions were around 3,350 m (length) × 210 m (breadth) × 60 m (depth). In the three days to 16 June the escape of water via the tunnel lowered the lake surface by nearly 14 m and reduced lake volume by about one-third. At the same time, it drastically reduced the length of the tunnel (and therefore the width of the ice dam) and also eroded soil underlying the dam. Not surprisingly, at this stage in the operation the water broke loose and the lake was emptied in half an hour. It was this outburst which devastated the Val de Bagnes and Martigny (Pictet 1819; Hall 1841; Mariétan 1959, 1970).

Despite the extent of destruction and death, Venetz's efforts simply cannot be dismissed as feeble or worthless. In the first place, it is obvious that the tragedy would have been much greater had he not intervened. The point was emphasized in a report made by Escher de la Linth shortly after the disaster. He estimated that if no tunnel had been dug, the volume of lake water would have increased to over three times the amount which had accumulated when the *débâcle* occurred. Furthermore, the outburst would have been delayed by about a month and this would have meant it pouring into the Rhône with the river level higher than when the actual flood took place. As a result, there would almost certainly have been widespread inundations between Martigny and Lake Geneva, whereas in reality this area escaped flooding (Mariétan 1959).

Any evaluation of Venetz's work must also take into account the way it stimulated efforts to find a solution to the Giétro problem. Thus, Escher de la Linth, in the report mentioned above, suggested that a tunnel be dug through the rocks of Mauvoisin, so that the Drance river could be diverted past any future ice dam. He thought this scheme should be financed from money which had been collected for the disaster victims. The idea was examined in detail by a commission, but was rejected because of technical difficulties. Also rejected was a proposal to construct an artificial lake at the base of the regenerated glacier. It was suggested that this would help melt the fallen ice, but the commission appeared to be more concerned about the lake freezing. Therefore, at this stage in discussions, its members were only able to advise that a careful watch be kept on the glacier and that, if necessary, the scheme which Venetz had adopted in 1818 be used again, though at an earlier stage of lake development. Fortunately, Venetz himself seemed eager to try new methods. Thus, he attempted to destroy or at least fracture the ice of the regenerated glacier with gunpowder. However, this did not prove too successful and was therefore abandoned. Venetz then had the idea of channelling water from nearby slopes on to the regenerated glacier, so that the ice could be melted and thereby divided into sections which were small enough to be carried away by the Drance river. Although this idea was far more successful, it still encountered difficulties. There was, for example, the problem of channelling water over the ice to exactly the spots where it would prove most effective, and there were dangers in actually having to work on the ice – Venetz was at one stage injured when he fell into a crevasse. Other difficulties were caused by J.-J. Blanc who maintained that the scheme was ineffective, though this view was challenged by several people. Writing in 1825, Blanc argued that diminution of the regenerated glacier since 1818 was attributable to natural processes rather than the work of Venetz. Whether or not this was true, the feature had shrunk even more by the 1840s and no longer constituted a source of danger. In 1842, Forbes described it as a 'very uninteresting looking glacier, which, in its present diminished form, scarcely attracts attention in the depth of the valley'. Yet, the impression left by the 1818 disaster was so great that work on melting the glacier continued. Forbes was therefore able to record that: 'When we passed the Glacier of Giétroz, there were workmen . . . dividing the ice into blocks, by the ingenious process of Venetz.' Later, in 1856, W. Mathews encountered 'a superintendent of the workmen who are constantly engaged in cutting away the dangerous glacier of Gétroz'. Indeed, it was not until 1884 that the danger was eventually regarded as so small that the work could be discontinued (Venetz 1823; Forbes 1900; Mathews 1926; Mariétan 1959).

For many years thereafter the Giétro glacier posed little or no threat to the Val de Bagnes and Martigny. However, in 1947 the Mauvoisin hydroelectric scheme was conceived and this led to the building of a 237 m high arch-dam (the largest of its kind in Switzerland) between 1951 and 1957. The lake which this now impounds is 5 km long. Significantly, the dam is only 400 m downvalley from where the regenerated glacier used to accumulate. The relative positions of dam, lake and glacier are shown in an excellent photograph on p. 125 of Bachmann's *Glaciers des Alpes* (Bachmann 1979). From this it can be seen that ice which becomes detached from the glacier snout will fall into the lake and melt. Thus, while the lake exists there is no danger of a regenerated glacier forming nor of an old-style *débâcle*. Unfortunately, by siting the dam and lake in this position, man has simply exchanged one type of glacier hazard for another. The new danger is that ice may fall into the lake and create waves which would overtop the dam and cause flooding downvalley. In view of this, detailed studies of the Giétro glacier have been made since 1966. According to Mariétan (1959), the earliest accurate and regular measurements of the glacier's fluctuations only date from 1953, due to problems of accessibility. The record shows that from 1953 to 1965 there was a slow retreat, whereas more recently a pronounced advance has occurred, so justifying the decision to undertake detailed studies. These have included both yearly and monthly observations of glacier velocity and have entailed the building of special measuring equipment. Particularly critical is the time of high water in the reservoir and how this might relate to ice breaking away from the snout of the Giétro glacier. Investigations suggest that an ice fall of at least 750,000 m³ would be needed to produce waves which could overtop the dam and flood areas downvalley (H. Röthlisberger 1974).

The engineering and scientific work carried out in the Giétro region from 1818 onwards provides an excellent illustration of man's attempts to reduce hazards caused by glacier fluctuations. However, in no way does this example cover the full range of glacier hazards, nor does it encompass all the responses to the problem. This is clearly borne out when considering that other source of *débâcles* in the Val de Bagnes, the Crête Sèche and Otemma glaciers. After the outburst from this source in 1894, a project was examined which would have involved digging a trench across the dike impounding the lake, so that dangerous accumulations of water could be prevented. The idea was, however, rejected because it would have meant excavating a great deal of material at a high cost. Further *débâcles* in 1895 and 1896 nevertheless convinced people that something must be done. Therefore, in 1897 large blocks were placed at the outlet in the dike through which the water was escaping. These were supposed to form a kind of riddle which would allow the water to drain away gradually, thus preventing the formation of a lake due to blocking of the outlet by snow and ice. Unfortunately, this scheme created precisely the situation it was intended to avoid. Fine snow closed the gaps between the blocks and frost solidified the whole mass. A lake formed once more and when the 'riddle' gave way, on 17 July 1898, the flood was even more destructive than its predecessors. In an effort to solve the problem, engineers reverted to the original scheme of excavating a trench across the dike to promote escape of lake water. The work was duly accomplished and the trench functioned as required for about ten years. By 1909, however, it was felt that all danger had passed and that an annual inspection of the situation would suffice. There the matter rested until 1926 when it was noted that the lake had re-formed after a very snowy winter and a relatively cold spring and summer. At first this provoked little concern, but when the lake continued to rise it became apparent that measures would have to be taken to prevent another *débâcle*. The scheme which was finally adopted bore a close resemblance to that devised in 1818 by Venetz. Thus, on both occasions, signalling posts were established to transmit the flood warning downvalley. In 1818 this was done using bonfires, whereas in 1926 the plan was to relay the warning from Crête Sèche to Fionnay by a series of explosions and thereafter to use the telephone. Both schemes involved digging an outlet through the barrier to facilitate escape of lake water. However, the 1818 outlet was excavated across a poorly consolidated regenerated glacier, while that of 1926 was dug in old ice, which was more compact and less likely to give way. This principally explains why the 1926 scheme was more successful. On that occasion, it took from 7 to 13 July to excavate a 200 m long trench across the barrier and from 13 July to 3 August for the lake to be drained, chiefly via this outlet. One million m³ of water were thereby released without causing damage (Mercanton 1899, 1928; Mariétan 1927a, 1959).

Since 1926 the moraine–ice barrier has gradually disappeared, so there now seems little danger of another *débâcle* from the Crête Sèche–Otemma region. Even were such an event to recur its impact would no doubt be minimal. This is because the flood would probably be 'absorbed' downstream by the Lac de Mauvoisin, especially if it occurred when the lake was low. Hence, such a *débâcle* would be unlikely to reach the lower, inhabited parts of the Val de Bagnes.

According to Mariétan (1927a), the Créte Sèche floods were similar to those from the Märjelensee, as both originated in lakes impounded at the flank of a glacier. However, the barrier at Crête Sèche was formed by a lateral moraine of the Otemma glacier, while the Märjelensee was dammed by the Aletsch glacier itself. Furthermore, the Crête Sèche *débâcles* occurred when glaciers were retreating from their Little Ice Age positions, while the Märjelensee floods were more dangerous when the Aletsch glacier was in an expanded state and was therefore able to dam the lake with a high wall of ice. Recent glacier shrinkage has not only lowered the height of this wall, but has consequently reduced the size of the lake which it can retain. In addition, man has attempted to lessen the hazard by providing the lake with an artificial outlet. The first to suggest this was Venetz who began examining the problem in the 1820s. Having realized it would be impracticable to dig an outlet across the glacier, because the ice barrier rose too far above lake level, he proposed excavating in the opposite direction.

His intention was to dig a trench in soil across a low col, so that excess water from the Märjelensee could escape into the Fiesch valley, hopefully without causing damage. Local inhabitants protested vigorously against the scheme, partly because they were worried that their cattle might be injured by falling into the trench, especially at night. They also complained that the scheme would cause their *alpage* to suffer from drought and that the *bisses* of Fiesch and Lax would receive less water. However, their fears were deemed to be groundless, so permission was given for work to start in 1828. When completed the following year, the trench had a length of 80 m and a depth of 3.8 m. On several later occasions inhabitants of the Fiesch valley complained of damage to their bridges from the water which the trench was carrying. Although they were doubtless exaggerating the problem, outbursts from the Märjelensee remained a hazard. Therefore, in 1881, some years after Venetz's death, it was decided to construct a 550 m long tunnel running in the same general direction as the trench, but at a lower level. Thus it was hoped that an even greater amount of lake water could be drained away. Regardless of fresh opposition by local inhabitants, the scheme was completed in 1894. Significantly, the only occasion when the tunnel functioned was for a period of about six weeks in 1896. Thereafter, the shrunken state of the Aletsch has ensured that the lake cannot rise to the tunnel entrance. Although *débâcles* have occurred since 1896, their generally reduced size has meant that they have become less of a problem. In addition, the likelihood that they would cause flooding has decreased owing to the construction since the 1850s of retaining embankments along many stretches of the Rhône river upstream from Lake Geneva. No doubt, in future the Aletsch glacier will again expand to its Little Ice Age dimensions. Under such circumstances the size of the Märjelensee will tend to increase, but will fail to attain its Little Ice Age extent, if the tunnel built in the 1890s can be made functional (Preller 1896a; Mariétan 1959; Aubert 1980).

A few years after completing the Märjelensee outlet, Venetz turned to the problems caused by the lake of Mattmark. The long history of *débâcles* from this source made it essential that the hazard be reduced. Venetz therefore undertook to excavate a relief channel across the ice and moraine of the Allalin glacier which was damming the Mattmarksee. This he did in 1834 and so caused the lake to shrink – by 1848, for example, its size was one-third less. As at Crête Sèche, the plan largely worked because the trench was excavated in compact ice. Though most Valaisan glaciers began a fairly persistent retreat after the mid nineteenth century, the terminus of the Allalin fluctuated somewhat erratically. Its retreat was therefore punctuated by advances. Because of this and the possible recurrence of lake formation and *débâcles*, it was suggested in 1905 that an overflow tunnel be built in the right-hand side of the valley. Two years later construction of this tunnel was approved, but the work did not actually take place until 1925/26, after a period (1915–23) when the tongue of the Allalin advanced 121 m and again blocked the Saastal (Lütschg 1926; Mariétan 1959; Bachmann 1979; Ruppen, Imseng and Imseng 1979).

Forty years later, when 1 million tons of ice crashed on to the huts of the workmen who were building the Mattmark dam, it was obvious that the nature of the hazards posed by the Allalin glacier had dramatically changed. The dam itself, by being located just upstream of where the glacier used to emerge from its side valley, ponds back the waters of the Saaser Vispa far more safely than did the barrier of ice and moraine. A dam-burst flood is therefore most unlikely. On the other hand, because the Allalin has retreated from the floor of the Saastal up a steep slope into its tributary valley, there is the new danger that parts of its terminal area might break away and avalanche down that slope. Such a danger has possibly existed several times before, when the Allalin has been in a contracted state. The 1965 avalanche had such tragic results merely because it destroyed temporary buildings which were full of workers. These had been located where it was thought they would not be at risk from snow avalanches. Although some ice had broken away from the Allalin in 1949, 1954, 1961 and 1963, no one had foreseen that the site was exposed to a major glacier avalanche. Fortunately, a tragedy similar to that of 1965 will probably never be repeated, as the Mattmark scheme is now finished and the workmen have left. If, however, there was a marked advance of the region's glaciers, new problems might arise – the Allalin would expand into the Saastal just downvalley from the dam and the Schwarzberg glacier would enter the reservoir (Bachmann 1979).

The psychological impact of the Allalin disaster was such that intensive scientific investigations of the glacier's behaviour were in progress even before the salvage work was finished. A programme of measurements was initiated which relied heavily on the use of aerial photographs. This revealed that in the second week after the disaster some parts of the glacier were moving as much as 3.5 m/day (Fig. 7.1). During the following week increased speeds of up to 6 m/day were recorded. Other useful data were obtained from photographs of the building site taken shortly before the disaster. These have the Allalin glacier in the background and show that during this period movement of its terminal area quickened to speeds of 1–2 m/day (H. Röthlisberger 1974).

Investigations of the Allalin have continued since 1965 and have uncovered a pattern of glacier behaviour. This consists of phases, when the ice moves only a few centimetres per day, broken every one to three years by periods of surge-like activity, during which velocity increases perhaps a hundredfold. Rapid movements of this sort are mainly confined to the second half of the year and arise due to availability of meltwater and the distribution of mass within the glacier. Surge-like activity was clearly required to produce the 1965 avalanche, but additional processes, such as the formation and collapse of a dome-shaped cavity, were needed for the event to be triggered off. Surges comparable to those of the Allalin have been observed elsewhere in the Saastal (e.g. on the Hohlaub and Trift glaciers) (H. Röthlisberger 1974, 1977).

Further investigations of the glacier problem in the Saastal have been carried out since 1969 with a view to protecting Saas Balen from débâcles of the Gruben ice-dammed lake. An understanding of this particular danger was helped by the occurrence in 1970 of a débâcle which it was possible to study in detail. Also at this time, work began on constructing an outflow for the lake. However, by 1973 this was encountering problems, so further work has been necessary to ensure that harmful débâcles will not occur in future. When the Saaser Chronik was published in 1979, this work was still incomplete (H. Röthlisberger 1974; Ruppen, Imseng and Imseng 1979).

The Bies glacier which hangs threateningly above Randa has also been investigated scientifically. In 1972 it was realized that the danger from this glacier was increasing, so a research programme was initiated. The danger arose because crevasses had opened where the glacier was on a 45° slope: this made it likely that part of the ice would become detached, thus producing an avalanche. Using several techniques (photography, lasers, etc.), research has shown that displacements were only a few centimetres per day in 1972, but increased sharply during 1973. As a result, in August of that year 500,000 m³ of ice became detached from the glacier. Fortunately for Randa, this development occurred in three phases and took several days: the ice therefore did not avalanche into the valley bottom, nor did it cause damage. In 1980, however, part of the Bies glacier did fall into the valley bottom, overwhelming the Visp–Zermatt railway line and blocking the Matter Vispa river (plate 6, p. 73). The lake which resulted was drained partly by cutting a relief channel similar to those

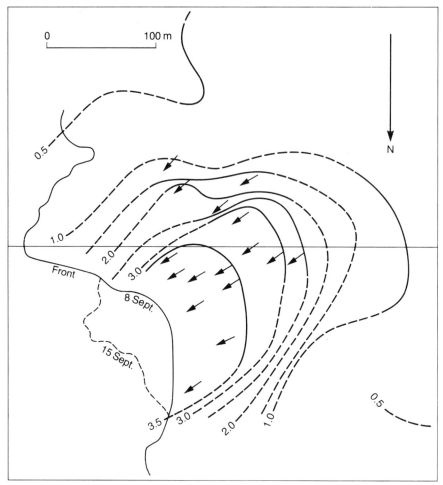

Fig 7.1 Allalin glacier: rates of movement (in metres) during the second week after the ice avalanche disaster of 1965. (After Röthlisberger, 1974).

made by Venetz in the first half of the nineteenth century, though on this occasion the task was easier and quicker due to the use of modern machinery. A familiar suggestion was made by a local dignitary to the effect that a covered overflow should be provided for the water to pass through if the avalanche again blocked the river channel (H. Röthlisberger 1974, 1977; Flotron 1977; Bachmann 1979; *Nouvelliste et Feuille d'Avis du Valais*, 7 and 8 February 1980).

In many cases, glacier hazards are best reduced by undertaking scientific and practical work on or near the offending glacier. However, where such hazards are likely to extend their influence well downvalley, as is the case particularly with *débâcles*, the embanking of streams is highly desirable. Venetz realized this when proposing the embankment and regulation of the Drance river, shortly after the Giétro flood of 1818. Similar work along the Rhône has likewise reduced the impact of *débâcles*, such as those originating from the Märjelensee. At present, the embanking and correction of the Fällbach, a stream issuing from the Gruben glacier, is helping to reduce the dangers from that source (Mariétan 1959; Ruppen, Imseng and Imseng 1979).

Avoiding the problem

Sometimes, man's response to glacier hazards in Valais has been to try and avoid them. For example, after the 1819 disaster at Randa, Venetz proposed abandoning the village and relocating it in a safer place a few kilometres upstream: such a move has, however, not been undertaken (Mariétan 1959). A modern equivalent of this proposal is that Randa should be evacuated when observations indicate a marked acceleration of movement on the Bies glacier (H. Röthlisberger 1974).

Another instance of how to avoid glacier hazards was seen by Lyell when he visited the Zermatt area in 1857. After commenting on the expansion of the Gorner glacier, he noted how the owners of chalets 'usually remove most of the woodwork before the ice comes and shoves the moraines against them' (Lyell 1881). However, if the literature is an accurate guide, this means of avoiding the full effects of ice expansion was not widely used, for there are numerous reports of chalet debris being ejected from glacier termini. By destroying homes and fields, expanding glaciers clearly brought about population migration, as also did the associated harsh climates. Thus, as the Gorner glacier advanced towards Zermatt, crop failures increased and starvation became widespread. To avoid this problem, many people left the area (Lehner, no date). The same thing happened in the Saastal following *débâcles* of the Mattmarksee. For example, in 1633, one such flood destroyed 18 houses and 6,000 trees, and spoiled much land: consequently, many people left for other parts of Switzerland or even abroad (Lütschg 1926; Ruppen, Imseng and Imseng 1979).

The avoidance of glacier hazards is also possible by realigning communication routes. When Valaisan glaciers expanded during the Little Ice Age some interfered with once-frequented mountain routes. Understandably, moves were made to develop new ways across the mountains or to improve those routes which were not affected by glaciers. Thus, Napoleon's development of the ice-free Simplon and Great St Bernard passes helped complete the decline of those routes in the intervening area (Theodul pass, Monte Moro pass, etc.) which had become difficult owing to glacier expansion. In the same way, the Lötschberg railway and tunnel have replaced the old high-level Lötschen pass (Harriss 1970, 1972).

Conclusions

There have been three phases in man's response to the hazards caused by Valaisan glaciers. During the earliest of these, it was thought that religious acts would induce the Almighty to quell such hazards. However, divine intervention turned out to be notoriously unreliable, so people began to look for other solutions. Inspired chiefly by Venetz, they gradually adopted a more practical attitude and this met with greater success. Indeed, some of Venetz's techniques are still in use today. For example, constructing an outlet trench helped reduce the impact of a glacier hazard at Randa as recently as 1980. In the current, third phase, man is developing a more scientific approach to the understanding and control of glacier behaviour. New methods of surveillance are being tried and these are producing a reorientation of the approach to glacier hazards in Valais. Whereas formerly man often responded to such hazards after they had occurred, careful scientific investigations are enabling him to predict glacier behaviour more accurately and so make it possible to take appropriate measures in the early stages of hazard development.

CHAPTER 8
GLACIERS AND PEOPLE IN VALAIS: THE FUTURE

Scenarios for the future

It might appear to some people that the glaciers of Valais are dying, for they have shrunk dramatically in the last 120 years. Yet, to imagine that they are all about to vanish is most unrealistic – for this to happen it would require a climatic change greater than any that has occurred during historic times, though some would argue the contentious point that just such a change will eventually be achieved by the man-induced build-up of atmospheric carbon dioxide. However, since about 1940 many parts of the world have experienced a temperature decline which has persisted longer than any similar trend during the last 200 years (Lamb 1977). It is also unrealistic to suggest that Valaisan glaciers will stay at about their present positions for an appreciable length of time. Stability has never been a characteristic of glaciers in the past, nor has it been typical of climate by which they are so markedly influenced. On the contrary, modern research is tending to emphasize the instability of the climatic and glacial environments.

More likely than the preceding scenarios is that Valaisan glaciers will return to something approaching their Little Ice Age positions. Yet, if it is correct that the Little Ice Age was not unique and that the expansion of its glaciers was matched or even surpassed a number of times during recent millennia, there must be a possibility that the next cold period might see a somewhat greater development of glaciers with all the problems which that would entail. These, however, would pale into insignificance were the idea of a 'snowblitz' to become reality. The widespread and rapid onset of glaciation which this theory proposes (Calder 1974; Gribbin 1976) has never occurred during historic times and for that reason has hardly been mentioned in preceding chapters. It should, nevertheless, be considered as a possible scenario for the future, if only because its implications for mankind are greater than those suggested by other predictions.

Problems

Scenarios of the kind just mentioned appear to have provoked little interest in Valais. Due to the resultant absence of a positive, forward-looking approach, man's response to glacier hazards within the canton has been generally piecemeal, often restrospective and largely unplanned. Many problems have therefore arisen and will continue to arise in future. Because it is unlikely that Valaisan glaciers will disappear or remain stable in the near future, there can be few grounds for expecting that the associated hazards will operate at a low and easily containable level of nuisance. In fact, the not unlikely scenario of glaciers returning to their maximum Little Ice Age positions would cause a variety of man-made structures to be damaged or destroyed. This would happen because glacier retreat since the mid nineteenth century has lured man into occupying areas which have only recently been vacated by the ice. When the greatest Little Ice Age extent of Valaisan glaciers is plotted on a map showing man-made structures, it becomes clear that the things at risk are of widely varying importance. The most serious dislocation would probably be that caused to the massive Grande Dixence hydroelectric scheme. In the Arolla valley, for example, one of the intakes for this scheme is only a very few minutes walk from an advancing glacier. Moreover, should this glacier and the nearby Tsidjiore Nouve regain their early nineteenth-century dimensions, a large pumping station and adjacent workmen's huts would also be at risk. If, however, Valaisan glaciers were to extend somewhat beyond their Little Ice Age maxima, a number of settlements would inevitably be damaged or destroyed. They would include not only small clusters of buildings, like those at Salay in the Ferpècle valley, but also places of importance, such as Arolla and Gletsch. More significant would be the impact of such an advance on Zermatt and Saas-Fee. Recent development of these well-known tourist centres has been partly towards glaciers which approached them closely at the Little Ice Age maxima. If in future these glaciers do no more than advance to within a short distance of the settlements, they might well be regarded as a tourist asset. This would cease to be the case were glacier damage to be in prospect or were life to be threatened. Difficulties would also be caused by Valaisan glaciers overrunning fields and roads, destroying trees and blocking streams; furthermore, there would be an increasing tendency for some glaciers to avalanche. Even so, things might still be a little better than during previous glacial maxima, since the availability of food is no longer dependent on what can be grown locally. However, this fact would be of little consequence for the people of Valais were a 'snowblitz' to develop. Not only would this submerge most of the canton beneath ice, it might also affect large areas of the Swiss Jura and Plateau.

The search for solutions

Today, most people seem to regard Valaisan glaciers as an unimportant hazard, particularly in view of their shrinkage during the last 120 years. Yet, to think that the problem can be virtually ignored is a most dangerous form of complacency. The present diminished state of Valaisan glaciers should, in fact, be looked upon as offering a breathing space during which new responses to the problem can be developed. If this opportunity is taken, man will be better equipped to cope with any future hazards which those glaciers might pose.

Of the scenarios described above, all but the 'snowblitz' can be planned for in a familiar way. Replacement of the piecemeal approach by a widely co-ordinated and planned response constitutes the single most important means of reducing the glacier problem in Valais. Such a response can be based on two things:

(a) Glacier surveillance: the current Swiss network of observations does not embrace all Valaisan glaciers, nor does it ensure that fluctuations will be measured accurately or regularly even when a glacier is listed as being studied. Furthermore, in most cases it is only variations of length which are recorded. The chief exceptions to this are the more detailed observations being carried out in the Aletsch and

Gries regions and on a small number of glaciers which have been identified as dangerous (e.g. the Giétro and Bies glaciers). Although the network for observing Swiss glacier fluctuations was established 100 years ago and has subsequently undergone many modifications, there are still aspects of glacier behaviour which escape regular and frequent study (Kasser and Aellen 1976). Therefore, unless the level of surveillance is improved, further glacier tragedies will occur in Valais and these may be no more expected than was the Allalin disaster of 1965.

The greater knowledge which would result from better levels of surveillance needs to be backed by a commensurate practical response. Especially encouraging is the discovery that the movements of some Valaisan glaciers follow a pattern. This obviously facilitates prediction of glacier behaviour and the implementation of measures necessary to protect people and property. Even if such patterns cannot be detected, careful surveillance must inevitably lead to a better understanding of glacier behaviour and an improved ability to contain any hazard this is likely to pose.

(b) Incorporation of glacier hazard data into the planning process: throughout most of historical time people have understood little of the dangers which Valaisan glaciers can provoke. This has led them to make unwise decisions in the siting of property, a classic example being the location of Randa. To try and reduce the problems caused by these mistakes, it has been necessary to undertake protective measures and careful glacier surveillance. If further problems are to be avoided, new building developments must be planned in such a way that they receive the minimum exposure to glacier hazards during their intended life span. The principle of zoning, which has become part of land-use planning in regions frequented by snow avalanches, might also be used, with appropriate modifications, where localities experience glacier danger. Its adoption would first of all require a thorough knowledge of past glacier catastrophes in Valais, an assessment of present dangers and, preferably, the compilation of glacier hazard maps. Such information would then provide the basis for land-use planning decisions in areas thought to be at risk. On the whole, low-cost, temporary and unimportant structures could be placed near to glaciers and in zones with a fair degree of risk from glacier floods or ice avalanches. More expensive, longer-lasting and sophisticated developments would have to be located further from glaciers in areas where the risk was deemed to be minimal or non-existent. It would, of course, be necessary to draw up specific technical and legal guidelines before such a scheme could be put into practice. However, as a number of developments have already taken place in areas of Valais at risk from glacier hazards, the introduction there of a zoning plan might be less valuable than in those regions of the world where such developments have not yet occurred.

Despite its merits, a planned response to glacier hazards does not constitute a perfect answer to the problem. Above all, such planning relies on the assumption that an unavoidably incomplete knowledge of past events is a sound basis for predicting how glaciers will affect man in the future. This assumption is questionable not only due to that incomplete knowledge, but also because the future may witness situations which have no previous parallel. These are more likely to arise from man's further development of areas prone to glacier hazards, rather than from an unusually marked glacier advance: the point is seemingly confirmed by hydroelectric projects which have been built close to the Giétro and Allalin glaciers. Owing to such difficulties, the idea of controlling glacier fluctuations becomes attractive. In a small, rather unintentional way, man has already begun to do this by constructing reservoirs immediately downstream of some Valaisan glaciers. However, future work might be better directed towards stabilizing or reducing glacier dimensions through artificial removal of their terminal extremities or their snow accumulation. Such an approach would be not unlike that used by Venetz and others in the nineteenth century for disposing of the ice which kept accumulating below the Giétro glacier and threatened to block the Drance river. Unfortunately, even this work would not eliminate all problems, because it would still be necessary to contend with the harsh climate which was provoking the glacier advance.

Concluding remarks

This book has been largely concerned with discovering how glacier fluctuations have affected man, particularly in the European Alps. The final two chapters nevertheless widen the scope of inquiry by examining man's response to glacier hazards in Valais and by considering future scenarios for this area. A detailed knowledge of past events is obviously important for understanding glacier fluctuations, but it is equally clear from the discussion of future scenarios that great efforts are needed to improve techniques for predicting and preventing glacier hazards both in Valais and elsewhere.

As there are many gaps in our knowledge, it is probably wise to treat glaciers with mistrust and suspicion. Consequently, any view which maintains that they are innocuous is untenable and must be abandoned not only by scientists and planners, but by the general public as well. In particular, it should never be forgotten that a glacier which at present may seem quiescent can rapidly become destructive and lethal as a result of a small climatic change.

REFERENCES

Agassiz, L. (1967) *Studies on glaciers preceded by the discourse of Neuchâtel*. Hafner, New York and London.

Ahlmann, H. W. and Thorarinsson, S. (1937) Vatnajökull: scientific results of the Swedish–Icelandic investigations 1936–37 (Ch. I–IV), *Geog. Annaler* **19**, 146–231.

Andrews, J. T. and Webber, P. J. (1969) Lichenometry to evaluate changes in glacier mass budgets: as illustrated from north-central Baffin Island, N.W.T., *Arctic and Alpine Research* **1**, 181–94.

Anon. (1673–74) A farther description and representation of the Icy Mountain, called the Gletscher, in the Canton of Berne in Helvetia: which was formerly taken notice of in Numb, 49 of these Tracts. *Philosophical Transactions of the Royal Society* **100**, 6191–2.

Aubert, D. (1980) Les stades de retrait des glaciers du Haut-Valais, *Bull. Murithienne* **97**, 101–69.

Bachmann, R. C. (1979) *Glaciers des Alpes*. Editions Payot, Lausanne.

Ball, J. (1875) *Bernese Alps including the Oberland* (*Ball's Alpine Guides*). Longmans, Green and Co., London.

Ball, J. (1878) *Pennine Alps including Mont Blanc and Monte Rosa* (*Ball's Alpine Guides*). Longmans, Green and Co., London.

Belloni, S. (1970) Nota preliminare sulle ricerche lichenometriche nell'alveo vallivo del ghiacciaio dei Forni, *Boll. Comitato Glaciologico Italiano* **18**, 1–8.

Belloni, S. (1973) Ricerche lichenometriche in Valfurva e nella valle di Solda, *Boll. Comitato Glaciologico Italiano* **21**, 19–33.

Benedict, J. B. (1967) Recent glacial history of an alpine area in the Colorado Front Range, USA. I. Establishing a lichen-growth curve, *Jour. Glaciology* **6**, 817–32.

Bérard, C. (1976) *Bataille pour l'eau* (2nd edn). Edition Monographic, Sierre.

Beschel, R. E. (1973) Lichens as a measure of the age of recent moraines, *Arctic and Alpine Research* **5**, 303–9.

Bezinge, A. (1966) *Grande Dixence et les problèmes météorologiques qui lui sont liés*, 9ᵉ Congrès international de météorologie alpine à Brigue et Zermatt, 14–17 septembre 1966.

Bezinge, A. (1971) *Déglaciation dans les vals de Zermatt et d'Hérens de 1930 à 1970*, Section de Glaciologie, Séance de Grenoble, 4–5 mars 1971.

Bezinge, A. (1978) *Torrents glaciaires: hydrologie et charriages d'alluvions*. Société Suisse des Sciences Naturelles, Assemblée annuelle Brigue, 5–8 octobre 1978.

Bezinge, A. and Bonvin, G. (1974) Images du climat sur les Alpes, *Bull. Murithienne* **91**, 27–48.

Bezinge, A., Perreten, J. P. and Schafer, F. (1973) Phénomènes du lac glaciaire du Gorner, in *Symposium on the Hydrology of Glaciers*, Cambridge, **7–13** 65–78, September 1969. Publication no. 95 of the International Association of Scientific Hydrology.

Bezinge, A. and Vivian, R. (1976) *Bilan de la Section de Glaciologie de la Société Hydrotechnique de France: sites sous-glaciaires et climat de la période holocène en Europe*, La Houille Blanche **6/7**, 441–60.

Blanchard, R. (1913) La crue glaciaire dans les Alpes de Savoie au XVIIᵉ siècle, *Recueil de travaux de l'Institut de géographie alpine* **1**, 443–54.

Bolt, B. A. *et al.* (1975) *Geological hazards*. Springer-Verlag, Berlin, Heidelberg, New York.

Bonney, T. G. (1887) The Märjalen See, *Nature* **36**, 612–13.

Bonney, T. G. (1902) Moraines and mud-streams in the Alps, *Geol. Magazine* **9**, 8–16.

Bonney, T. G. (1912) *The building of the Alps*. T. F. Unwin, London.

Bourrit, M.-T. (1787) *Nouvelle description des glacières, vallées de glace et glaciers qui forment la grande chaine des Alpes, de Savoye, de Suisse et d'Italie*. Barde, Manget & Comp., Geneva (reprinted 1981 by Editions Slatkine, Geneva).

Bowen, D. Q. (1977) Hot and cold climates in prehistoric Britain, *Geog. Magazine* **49**, 685–98.

Bryson, R. A. and Murray, T. J. (1977) *Climates of hunger*. University of Wisconsin Press.

Buhrer, C. (1904) Les variations de climat dans les Alpes spécialement dans le Valais, *Bull. Murithienne* **33**, 168–203.

Burrows, C. J. and Orwin, J. (1971) Studies on some glacial moraines in New Zealand. 1. The establishment of lichen-growth curves in the Mount Cook area, *New Zealand Jour. Science* **14**, 327–35.

Calder, N. (1974) *The weather machine and the threat of ice*. British Broadcasting Corporation, London.

Castiglioni, G. B. (ed.) (1974) *Le calamità naturali nelle Alpi*. Istituto di Geografia dell'Università di Padova.

Coates, D. R. (ed.) (1971) *Environmental geomorphology*. Publications in Geomorphology, State University of New York, Binghamton, New York.

Coaz, J. (1881) *Die Lauinen der Schweizeralpen*. Berne.

Colbeck, S. C. (1974) A study of glacier flow for an open-pit mine: an exercise in applied glaciology, *Jour. Glaciology* **13**, 401–14.

Collet, L. W. (1926) The lakes of Scotland and of Switzerland, *Geog. Jour.* **67**, 193–213.

Collingwood, W. G. (1884) *The limestone Alps of Savoy; a study in physical geology*. G. Allen, Orpington, Kent.

Collomb, E. (1857) *Mémoire sur les glaciers actuels*. V. Dalmont, Paris.

Coolidge, W. A. B. (1908) *The Alps in nature and history*. Methuen & Co., London.

Cooper, W. S. (1937) The problem of Glacier Bay, Alaska: a study of glacier variations, *Geog. Review* **27**, 37–62.

Croot, D. G. and Escritt, E. A. (1976) Scourge of surging glaciers, *Geog. Magazine* **48**, 328–34.

De Beer, G. R. (1950) Johann Heinrich Hottinger's description of the ice-mountains of Switzerland, 1703, *Annals of Science* **6**, 327–60.

De Beer, G. (1967) *Early travellers in the Alps*. October House, New York.

Denton, G. H. (1975a) Canadian Rocky Mountains, in W. O. Field (ed.), *Mountain glaciers of the northern hemisphere*, vol. 1, part VI, Ch. 1. Cold Regions Research and Engineering Laboratory, Hanover, New Hampshire, USA.

Denton, G. H. (1975b) Iceland, in 'W. O. Field (ed.), *Mountain glaciers of the northern hemisphere*, vol. 2, part IX, Ch. 3. Cold Regions Research and Engineering Laboratory, Hanover, New Hampshire, USA.

Denton, G. H. and Karlén, W. (1973) Lichenometry: its application to Holocene moraine studies in Southern Alaska and Swedish Lapland, *Arctic and Alpine Research* **5**, 347–72.

Derbyshire, E. and Miller, K. (1981) Highway beneath the Ghulkin, *Geog. Magazine* **53**, 626–35.

Desio, A. (1954) An exceptional glacier advance in the Karakoram–Ladakh region, *Jour. Glaciology* **2**, 383–5.

Dury, G. H. (1960) *The face of the Earth*. Penguin Books, Harmondsworth, Middlesex.

Eckel, E. B. (1970) The Alaska earthquake March 27, 1964: lessons and conclusions. *United States Geological Survey*, Professional Paper 546.

Eythorsson J. (1935) On the variations of glaciers in Iceland. Some studies made in 1931, *Geog. Annaler* **17**, 121–37.

Falconer, G. (1966) Preservation of vegetation and patterned ground under a thin ice body in northern Baffin Island, NWT, *Geog. Bulletin* **8**, 194–200.

Field, W. O. (1975a) Introduction, in W. O. Field (ed.), *Mountain glaciers of the northern hemisphere*, vol. 1, Cold Regions Research and Engineering Laboratory, Hanover, New Hampshire, USA.

Field, W. O. (1975b) Glaciers of the Chugach Mountains, in W. O. Field (ed.), *Mountain glaciers of the northern hemisphere*, vol. 2, part VII, ch. 3. Cold Regions Research and Engineering Laboratory, Hanover, New Hampshire, USA.

Finsterwalder, R. (1954) Photogrammetry and glacier research with special reference to glacier retreat in the eastern Alps, *Jour. Glaciology* **2**, 306–15.

Finsterwalder, R. (1960) German glaciological and geological expeditions to the Batura Mustagh and Rakaposhi range, *Jour. Glaciology* **3**, 787–8.

Flotron, A. (1977) Movement studies on a hanging glacier in relation with an ice avalanche, *Jour. Glaciology* **19**, 671–2.

Forbes, J. D. (1855) *The tour of Mont Blanc and of Monte Rosa.* A. and C. Black, Edinburgh.

Forbes, J. D. (1900) *Travels through the Alps.* New edition revised and annotated by W. A. B. Coolidge, A. and C. Black, London.

Forel, F.-A. (1888) Les variations périodiques des glaciers des Alpes, *Jahrb. Schweizer Alpenclub* **23**, 257–87.

Forel, F.-A. (1901) Petites crues apparaissant au milieu de la grande décrue des glaciers, *Jahrb. Schweizer Alpenclub* **36**, 169–73.

Fraser, C. (1966) *The avalanche enigma.* Murray, London.

Freeberne, M. (1965) Glacial meltwater resources in China, *Geog. Jour.* **131**, 57–60.

Glaister, R. M. (1951) The ice slide on the Glacier du Tour. *Jour. Glaciology* **9**, 508–9.

Godwin-Austen, H. H, (1864) On the glaciers of the Mustakh Range. *Jour. Royal Geog. Society* **34**, 19–56.

Gosset, P. (1888) Der Märjelensee, *Jahrb. Schweizer Alpenclub* **23**, 304–54.

Goudie, A. (1981) Fearful landscape of the Karakoram, *Geog. Magazine* **53**, 306–12.

Grant, U. S. and Higgins, D. F. (1913) Coastal glaciers of Prince William Sound and Kenai Peninsula, Alaska. *United States Geological Survey*, Bulletin 526, Washington.

Gribbin, J. (1976) *Forecasts, famines and freezes.* Wildwood House, London.

Grove, J. M. (1966) The Little Ice Age in the Massif of Mont Blanc, *Institute of British Geographers, Transactions* no. 40, 129–43.

Grove, J. M. (1972) The incidence of landslides, avalanches and floods in western Norway during the Little Ice Age, *Arctic and Alpine Research* **4**, 131–8.

Grove, J. M. (1979) The glacial history of the Holocene, *Progress in Physical Geography* **3**, 1–54.

Grove, J. M. and Battagel, A. (1981) Tax records as an index of Little Ice Age environmental and economic deterioration from Sunnfjord Fogderi, Norway, in C. D. Smith and M. Parry (eds), *Consequences of climatic change*, Dept. Geography, University of Nottingham.

Gutersohn, H. (1961) *Geographie der Schweiz* (vol. II, *Alpen*, Part I). Kümmerly and Frey, Geographischer Verlag, Berne.

Haefeli, R. (1963) Note on the history of the Steingletscher lake, *International Association of Scientific Hydrology Bulletin* **8**, 123–5.

Haefeli, R. (1966) Note sur la classification, le mécanisme et le contrôle des avalanches de glace et des crues glaciaires extraordinaires, in *International Symposium on Scientific Aspects of Snow and Ice Avalanches*, 5–10 April 1965, Davos, Switzerland. Publication no. 69 of the International Association of Hydrological Sciences, 316–25.

Hall, B. (1841) *Patchwork.* Second edn, vol. 1, E. Moxon, London.

Harriss, B. (1970) The Theodulpass: a history, *Alpine Jour.* **75**, 87–94.

Harriss, B. (1971) The Monte Moro pass and the Col d'Hérens, *Alpine Jour.* **76**, 127–32.

Harriss, B. (1972) Travel and trade in the Pennine Alps, *Alpine Jour.* **77**, 175–82.

Hastenrath, S. (1981) *The glaciation of the Ecuadorian Andes.* A. A. Balkema, Rotterdam.

Hayden, H. H. (1907) Notes on certain glaciers in north-west Kashmir, *Records of the Geol. Survey of India* **35**, 127–37.

Helbling, R. (1935) The origin of the Rio Plomo ice-dam, *Geog. Jour.* **85**, 41–9.

Heybrock, W. (1935) Earthquakes as a cause of glacier avalanches in the Caucasus, *Geog. Review* **25**, 423–9.

Hoel, A. and Werenskiold, W. (1962) Glaciers and snowfields in Norway, *Norsk Polarinstitutt Skrifter* **114**, 291.

Hoinkes, H. C. (1969) Surges of the Vernagtferner in the Ötztal Alps since 1599, *Canadian Jour. Earth Sciences* **6**, 853–61.

Holmes, A. (1965) *Principles of physical geology.* T. Nelson and Sons, London and Edinburgh.

Horvath, E. (1975) Glaciers of Pamir-Alay, in W. O. Field (ed.), *Mountain glaciers of the northern hemisphere, vol. 1, part II, Ch. 4.* Cold Regions Research and Engineering Laboratory, Hanover, New Hampshire, USA.

Horvath, E. and Field, W. O. (1975) Glaciers of the Kavkaz (Caucasus), in W. O. Field (ed.), *Mountain glaciers of the northern hemisphere*, vol. 1, part II, Ch. 3. Cold Regions Research and Engineering Laboratory, Hanover, New Hampshire, USA.

Husseiny, A. A. (ed.) (1978) *Iceberg utilization. Proceedings of the First International Conference and Workshops on Iceberg Utilization . . . 1977.* Pergamon Press, New York.

Ingram, M. J., Underhill, D. J. and Farmer G. (1981) The use of documentary sources for the study of past climates, in T. M. L. Wigley *et al*, (eds) *Climate and history: studies in past climates and their impact on Man.* Cambridge University Press.

Innes, J. L. (1981) 'A manual for lichenometry' – comment, *Area* **13**, 237–41.

Jackson, L. E. (1979) A catastrophic glacial outburst flood (jökulhlaup) mechanism for debris flow generation at the Spiral Tunnels, Kicking Horse River basin, British Columbia, *Canadian Geotechnical Jour.* **16**, 806–13.

John, B. S. and Sugden, D. E. (1962) The morphology of Kaldalon, a recently deglaciated valley in Iceland, *Geog. Annaler* **44**, 347–65.

Karlén, W. (1973) Holocene glacier and climatic variations, Kebnekaise Mountains, Swedish Lapland, *Geog. Annaler* **55**, 29–63.

Kasser, P. (1967) *Fluctuations of glaciers 1959–1965* (vol. 1). International Commission of Snow and Ice of the International Association of Scientific Hydrology and UNESCO, Paris.

Kasser, P. (1973) *Fluctuations of glaciers 1965–1970* (vol. II). International Commission on Snow and Ice of the International Association of Hydrological Sciences and UNESCO, Paris.

Kasser, P. and Aellen, M. (1976) Les variations des glaciers suisses en 1974–1975 et quelques indications sur les résultats récoltés pendant la Décennie Hydrologique Internationale de 1964–65 à 1973–74, *La Houille Blanche* **6/7**, 467–80.

Kates, R. W. (1980) Climate and society: lessons from recent events, *Weather* **35**, 17–25.

Kick, W. (1966) Measuring and mapping of glacier variations, *Canadian Jour. Earth Sciences* **3**, 775–81.

King, W. D. V. O. (1934) The Mendoza river flood of 10–11 January 1934–Argentina, *Geog. Jour.* **84**, 321–6.

Konecny, G. (1966) Applications of photogrammetry to surveys of glaciers in Canada and Alaska, *Canadian Jour. Earth Sciences* **3**, 783–98.

Kotliakov, V. M. and Touchinski, G. K. (1974) Le régime actuel des glaciers et des avalanches dans le Caucase, *Revue de Géog. Physique et de Géol. Dynamique* **16**, 299–312.

Ladurie, E. le R. (1967) *Histoire du climat depuis l'an mil.* Flammarion, Paris.

Ladurie, E. le R. (1972) *Times of feast, times of famine: a history of climate since the year 1000.* G. Allen & Unwin, London.

Lamarche, V. C. and Fritts, H. C. (1971) Tree rings, glacial advance, and climate in the Alps. *Zeitschrift für Gletscherkunde und Glazialgeologie* **7**, 125–31.

Lamb, H. H. (1974) *The current trend of world climate – a report on the early 1970s and a perspective.* Climatic Research Unit, School of Environmental Sciences, University of East Anglia, Norwich.

Lamb, H. H. (1977) *Climate: present, past and future*, vol. 2, *Climatic history and the future.* Methuen and Co., London.

Lardy, C. (1836) Note sur l'éboulement d'une portion de la Dent du Midi, *Bull. Société Géol. France* **7**, 27–30.

Lawrence, D. B. (1950) Estimating dates of recent glacier advances and recession rates by studying tree growth layers, *Transactions, American Geophysical Union* **31**, 243–8.

Lehner, K. (no date) *A pocket history of Zermatt.* Neue Buchdruckerei Visp AG, Visp.

Lehr, P. and Horvath, E. (1975) Glaciers of China, in W. O. Field (ed.), *Mountain glaciers of the northern hemisphere*, vol. 1, part III, Ch. 5. Cold Regions Research and Engineering Laboratory, Hanover, New Hampshire, USA.

Liestøl, O. (1955) Glacier dammed lakes in Norway, *Norsk Geog. Tidsskrift* **15**, 122–49.

Lliboutry, L. (1971) Les catastrophes glaciaires, *La Recherche* **2**, 417–25.

Lliboutry, L. (1973) Observations de lacs proglaciaires dangereux dans la Cordillera Blanca (Pérou), in *Symposium on the Hydrology of Glaciers*, Cambridge, 7–13 September 1969. Publication no. 95 of the International Association of Hydrological Sciences, 135.

Lliboutry, L. A. (1975) Le catastrophe de Yungay (Pérou), in *Symposium on Snow and Ice*, Moscow, August 1971. Publication no. 104 of the International Association of Hydrological Sciences, 353–63.

Lliboutry, L. *et al.* (1977) Glaciological problems set by the control of dangerous lakes in Cordillera Blanca, Peru. I. Historical failures of morainic dams, their causes and prevention, *Jour. Glaciology* **18**, 239–54.

Longstaff, T. G. (1910) Glacier exploration in the Eastern Karakoram, *Geog. Jour.* **35**, 622–58.

Lüthi, A. (1978) *Zermatt und die Hochalpenpässe.* Buchdruckerei Tscherrig AG.

Lütschg, O. (1916) Les variations des glaciers d'Allalin et de Schwarzenberg, *Archives des Sciences Physiques et Naturelles* **42**, 503–5.

Lütschg, O. (1926) *Uber Niederschlag und Abfluss im Hochgebirge Sonderdarstellung des Mattmarkgebietes.* Schweizerischer Wasserwirtschaftsverband. Verbandsschrift Nr. 14. Veröffentlichung der Hydrologischen Abteilung der Schweizerischen Meteorologischen Zentralanstalt in Zürich.

Lyell, Mrs. (ed.) (1881) *Life, letters and journals of Sir Charles Lyell, Bart.* 2 vols, Murray, London.

McDowell, B. (1962) Avalanche! *National Geog.* **121**, 855–80.

Mariétan, I. (1927a) Les débâcles du glacier de Crête-Sèche (Bagnes), *Bull. Murithienne* **44**, 40–9.

Mariétan, I. (1927b) Les éboulements de la Cime de l'Est des Dents du Midi en 1926 et le Bois-Noir, *Bull. Murithienne* **44**, 67–93.

Mariétan, I. (1952) Stalden-St. Nicolas-Grächen-Eisten, *Bull. Murithienne* **69**, 110–13.

Mariétan, I. (1955) Notes sur la vallée de Conches, *Bull. Murithienne* **72**, 80–7.

Mariétan, I. (1959) La vie et l'oeuvre de l'ingénieur Ignace Venetz, *Bull. Murithienne* **76**, 1–51.

Mariétan, I. (1965) Mattmark et le glacier d'Allalin, *Bull. Murithienne* **82**, 129–48.

Mariétan, I. (1970) La catastrophe du Giétroz en 1818. Divers, *Bull. Murithienne* **87**, 12–19.

Martin-Chavannes, J. (1953) Les débâcles au vallon de Ferpècle, *Die Alpen* **29**, 26–9.

Mason, K. (1914) Examination of certain glacier snouts of Hunza and Nagar, *Records, Survey of India* **6**, 48–51.

Mason, K. (1929) Indus floods and Shyok glaciers, *Himalayan Jour.* **1**, 10–29.

Mason, K. (1935) The study of threatening glaciers, *Geog. Jour.* **85**, 24–41.

Mathews, W. (1926) The mountains of Bagnes, with the ascents of the Vélan, Combin, and Graffeneire, and the passage of the Col du Mont Rouge, in E. H. Blakeney (ed.), *Peaks, passes and glaciers*. J. M. Dent & Sons, London and Toronto.

Matthes, F. E. (1942) Glaciers, in O. E. Meinzer (ed.), *Hydrology*. Dover Publications, New York.

Matthews, J. A. (1977) Glacier and climatic fluctuations inferred from tree-growth variations over the last 250 years, central southern Norway, *Boreas* **6**, 1–24.

Mayr, F. (1968) Postglacial glacier fluctuations and correlative phenomena in the Stubai Mountains, Eastern Alps, Tyrol, in G. M. Richmond (ed.), *Glaciation of the Alps*. University of Colorado Press, Boulder, Colorado.

Mercanton, P. L. (1899) Les débâcles au glacier de Crête-Sèche, *Jahrb. Schweizer Alpenclub* **34**, 265–74.

Mercanton, P. L. (1928) Le lac temporaire du glacier de Crête-Sèche: à propos d'une menace récente, *Die Alpen* **4**, 214–16.

Mercanton, P. L. (1954) Glacierized areas in the Swiss Alps, *Jour. Glaciology* **2**, 315–16.

Mercer, J. H. (1975a) Glaciers of the Alps, in W. O. Field (ed.), vol. 1, part I, Ch. 2. *Mountain glaciers of the northern hemisphere*. Cold Regions Research and Engineering Laboratory, Hanover, New Hampshire, USA.

Mercer, J. H. (1975b) Glaciers of the Karakoram, in W. O. Field (ed.), *Mountain glaciers of the northern hemisphere*, vol. 1, part III, Ch. 3. Cold Regions Research and Engineering Laboratory, Hanover, New Hampshire, USA.

Mercer, J. H. (1975c) Glaciers of the Himalaya, in W. O. Field (ed.), *Mountain glaciers of the northern hemisphere*, vol. 1, part III, Ch. 4. Cold Regions Research and Engineering Laboratory, Hanover, New Hampshire, USA.

Messerli, B. *et al.* (1975) Die Schwankungen des Unteren Grindelwaldgletschers seit dem Mittelalter, *Zeitschrift für Gletscherkunde und Glazialgeologie* **11**, 3–110.

Messerli, B. *et al.* (1978) Fluctuations of climate and glaciers in the Bernese Oberland, Switzerland, and their geoecological significance, 1600 to 1975, *Arctic and Alpine Research* **10**, 247–60.

Miller, M. M. (1963) *The regional pattern of Alaskan glacier fluctuations (with some comments on the problems of earthquake avalanching and climatic change)*. Foundation for Glacier Research, Seattle, Washington.

Montandon, F. (1926) Note sur les coulées des 20 et 26 septembre 1926, au Bois Noir, et comparaison avec celles de 1835, *Die Alpen* **2**, 438–40.

Morales, B. (1966) The Huascaràn avalanche in the Santa valley, Peru, in *International Symposium on Scientific Aspects of Snow and Ice Avalanches*, 5–10 April 1965, Davos, Switzerland. Publication no. 69 of the International Association of Hydrological Sciences 304–15.

Moulinié, C. E. F. (1820) *Sermon prononcé à Genève, le 28 juin 1818, par le pasteur Moulinié, à l'occasion de l'inondation qui a désolé la vallée de Bagne et la ville de Martigny en Valais, le 16 du même mois*. Imprimerie de Luc Sestié et fils, Geneva.

Müller, F. (1977) *Fluctuations of glaciers 1970–1975* (vol. III). International Commission on Snow and Ice of the International Association of Hydrological Sciences and UNESCO, Paris.

Müller, H.-N. (1975) Fossile Böden (fAh) in Moränen (Gäli Egga, Rossbodengebiet, Simplon VS), *Bull. Murithienne* **92**, 21–31.

Muret, E. (1901) Les variations périodiques des glaciers spécialement en ce qui concerne les glaciers du Valais, *Murithienne, Société Valaisanne des Sciences Naturelles* **29–30**, 43–65.

Murray, J. (1829) *A glance at some of the beauties and sublimities of Switzerland.* Longman, Rees, Orme, Brown and Green, London.

Mutton, A. F. A. (1951) The Glockner–Kaprun hydroelectric project, Hohe Tauern, Austria, *Geog. Review* **41**, 332–4.

Nichols, R. L. and Miller, M. M. (1952) The Moreno glacier, Lago Argentino, Patagonia: advancing glaciers and nearby simultaneously retreating glaciers, *Jour. Glaciology* **2**, 41–50.

Ogilvie, A. E. J. (1981) Climate and economy in eighteenth century Iceland, in C. D. Smith and M. Parry (eds), *Consequences of climatic change.* Dept. Geography, University of Nottingham.

Østrem, G. (1972) Runoff forecasts for highly glacierized basins, *Proceedings of the Banff Symposium: Role of Snow and Ice in Hydrology.* UNESCO–WMO and IAHS.

Park, C. C. (1980) The Grande Dixence hydro-electric scheme, Switzerland, *Geography*, **65**, 317–20.

Partl, R. (1978) Power from Greenland's glaciers, *Water Power and Dam Construction* **30**, 42–50.

Paterson, W. S. B. (1981) *The physics of glaciers* (2nd edn). Pergamon Press, New York.

Péguy, Ch.–P. (1956) Centrales et glaciers du Grossglockner, *Revue de Géog. Alpine* **44**, 393–8.

Pictet, Professor (1819) Account of the formation of the Lake of Mauvoisin, by the descent of a glacier, and of the inundations of the Val de Bagnes in 1595 and 1818. Drawn up from the memoir of M. Escher de la Linth, &c, *Edinburgh Philosophical Jour.* **1**, 187–91.

Porter, S. C. (1981) Glaciological evidence of Holocene climatic change, in T. M. L. Wigley *et al.* (eds), *Climate and history: studies in past climates and their impact on man.* Cambridge University Press.

Preller, C. S. du R. (1896a) The Merjelen lake (Aletsch glacier), *Geol. Magazine* **3** (New series, decade IV), 97–102.

Preller, C. S. du R. (1896b) The ice-avalanche on the Gemmi Pass (Switzerland), *Geol. Magazine* **3** (New series, decade IV), 103–6.

Preusser, H. (1976) *The landscapes of Iceland: types and regions.* Dr. W. Junk b.v., The Hague.

Rabassa, J., Rubulis, S. and Suárez, J. (1979) Rate of formation and sedimentology of (1976–1978) push moraines, Frias Glacier, Mount Tronador (41° 10'S: 71° 53'W), Argentina, in Ch. Schlüchter (ed.) *Proceedings of an INQUA symposium on genesis and lithology of Quaternary deposits*, Zurich, 10–20 September 1978. A. A. Balkema, Rotterdam.

Rabot, C. (1905) Glacial reservoirs and their outburst, *Geog. Jour.* **25**, 534–48.

Rabot, C. (1920) Les catastrophes glaciaires dans la vallée de Chamonix au XVIIᵉ siècle et les variations climatiques, *La Nature* **46**, 129–34.

Renaud, A. (1963) Les glaciers de la région de Zermatt, *International Association of Scientific Hydrology Bulletin* **8**, 109–12.

Rendu, M. le Chanoine (1840) *Théorie des glaciers de la Savoie.* Puthod, Chambéry (translated into English by A. Wills, 1874, Macmillan and Co., London).

Reynolds, J. M. (1979) Icebergs are a frozen asset, *Geog. Magazine* **52**, 177–85.

Richardson, D. (1968) Glacier outburst floods in the Pacific Northwest. *United States Geol. Survey*, Professional Paper 600D, D79–D86.

Richardson, D. H. S. (1975) *The vanishing lichens.* David & Charles, Newton Abbot.

Richter, E. (1891) Geschichte der Schwankungen der Alpengletscher, *Zeitschrift des Deutschen und Oesterreichischen Alpenvereins* **22**, 1–74.

Roethlisberger, F. and Schneebeli, W. (1979) Genesis of lateral moraine complexes, demonstrated by fossil soils and trunks: indicators of postglacial climatic fluctuations, in Ch. Schlüchter (ed), *Proceedings of an INQUA symposium on genesis and lithology of Quaternary deposits, Zurich, 10–20 September 1978.* A. A. Balkema, Rotterdam.

Röthlisberger, F. (1974) Etude des variations climatiques d'après l'histoire des cols glaciaires. Le Col d'Hérens (Valais, Suisse), *Boll. Comitato Glaciologico Italiano* **22**, 9–34.

Röthlisberger, F. (1976) Gletscher- und Klimaschwankungen im Raum Zermatt, Ferpècle und Arolla, *Die Alpen* **52**, 59–152.

Röthlisberger, F. *et al.* (1980) Holocene climatic fluctuations – radiocarbon dating of fossil soils (fAh) and woods from moraines and glaciers in the Alps, *Geog. Helvetica* **35**, special issue, 21–52.

Röthlisberger, H. (1974) Möglichkeiten und Grenzen der Gletscherüberwachung, *Neue Zürcher Zeitung* **196**, 39–42.

Röthlisberger, H. (1977) Ice avalanches, *Jour. Glaciology* **19**, 669–71.

Rudolph, R. (1963) A brief account of the geography of the central Oetztal Alps with special reference to its glaciology, *International Association of Hydrological Sciences Bulletin* **8**, 126–31.

Rüegg, W. (1962) La Cordillère Blanche du Pérou et la catastrophe du Huascaran, *Die Alpen* **38**, 275–80.

Ruppen, P. J., Imseng, G. and Imseng, W. (1979) *Saaser Chronik 1200–1979*. Verkehrsverein, Saas-Fee.

Schardt, H. (1902) Avalanche du glacier du Rossboden (Simplon), *Eclogae Geol. Helvetiae* **7**, 347–50.

Schneebeli, W. (1976) Untersuchungen von Gletscherschwankungen im Val de Bagnes, *Die Alpen* **52**, 5–57.

Schomberg, R. (1934) The glaciers of Upper Ishkoman, *Alpine Jour.* **46**, 344–50.

Schwarzl, S. (1979) Die klimatischen Ursachen der extremen Gletschervorstösse Ende des 16. Jahrhunderts und der Niedergang des Goldbergbaues in den Rauriser Alpen (Hohe Tauern). Paper submitted to the *International Conference on Climate and History*, 8–14 July 1979, Climatic Research Unit, University of East Anglia, Norwich.

Sourbier, M. M. du (1950) Note sur l'éboulement du Glacier du Tour (Haute-Savoie) (14 août 1949), *Société Hydrotechnique de France, Mémoires et Travaux* **1**, 56–60.

Stone, K. H. (1963) Alaskan ice-dammed lakes, *Annals of the Association of American Geographers* **53**, 332–49.

Stork, A. (1963) Plant immigration in front of retreating glaciers, with examples from the Kebnekajse area, northern Sweden, *Geog. Annaler* **45**, 1–22.

Sugden, D. (1978) Extremes of a glacial planet, *Geog. Magazine* **51**, 119–28.

Theakstone, W. H. (1965) Recent changes in the glaciers of Svartisen, *Jour. Glaciology* **5**, 411–31.

Thorarinsson, S. (1939) The ice-dammed lakes of Iceland, with particular reference to their values as indicators of glacier oscillations, *Geog. Annaler* **21**, 216–42.

Thorarinsson, S. (1943) Vatnajökull. Scientific results of the Swedish–Icelandic investigations 1936–37–38. Ch. XI. Oscillations of the Iceland glaciers in the last 250 years, *Geog. Annaler* **25**, 1–54.

Thorarinsson, S. (1956) *The thousand years struggle against ice and fire*. Bókaútgáfa Menningarsjóds, Reykjavik.

Thorarinsson, S. (1957) The jökulhlaup from the Katla area in 1955 compared with other jökulhlaups in Iceland, *Jökull* **7**, 21–5.

Thorarinsson, S. (1958) The Öraefajökull eruption of 1362, *Acta Naturalia Islandica* **2**, 99.

Thorarinsson, S. (1960) Glaciological knowledge in Iceland before 1800, *Jökull* **10**, 1–18.

Thorarinsson, S. (1964) On the age of the terminal moraines of Brúarjökull and Hálsajökull: a tephrochronological study, *Jökull* **14**, 67–75.

Tollner, H. (1957) Die Folgen des Rückganges österreichischer Gletscher auf die Wasserspeicherung hochalpiner Kraftwerksanlagen, *Jahres. Sonnblick-Vereines* **51–3**, 38–42.

Tricart, J. (1970) *Geomorphology of cold environments*. Macmillan, London.

Tscheinen, M. (1860) Gletschersturz in Randa 1819, *Vierteljahrsschrift der Naturforschenden Gesellschaft in Zürich* **5**, 323–5.

Tufnell, L. (1980) Les catastrophes géomorphologiques en Valais, *Bull. Murithienne* **97**, 83–99.

Tyndall, J. (1911) *The glaciers of the Alps*. Longmans Green, London.

Vanni, M. (1966) Pour une classification géographique des avalanches, in *International Symposium on Scientific Aspects of Snow and Ice Avalanches*, 5–10 April 1965, Davos, Switzerland. Publication no. 69 of the International Association of Scientific Hydrology, 397–407.

Venetz, I. (1823) Rapport fait à la Société Helvétique d'Histoire naturelle, assemblée à Berne, le 24 juillet 1822, sur les travaux du glacier de Giétroz, *Naturwissenschaftlicher Anzeiger der allgemeinen Schweizerischen Gesellschaft für die gesammten Naturwissenschaften* **5**, 82–4.

Vincent, F. (1976) *Aspects de certains reliefs de la vallée de Chamonix*. Atelier Esope, Chamonix. Edition Association des Amis de la Réserve Naturelle des Aiguilles Rouges.

Viollet-le-Duc, E. (1877) *Mont Blanc, a treatise on its geodesical and geological constitution; its transformations; and the ancient and recent state of its glaciers*. Sampson Low, Marston, Searle & Rivington, London.

Vivian, R. (1966) La catastrophe du glacier Allalin, *Revue de Géog. Alpine* **54**, 97–112.

Vivian, R. (1971) Les variations récentes des glaciers dans les Alpes françaises (1900–1970): possibilités de prévision, *Revue de Géog. Alpine* **59**, 229–42.

Vivian, R. (1974) Les débâcles glaciaires dans les Alpes Occidentales, in G. B. Castiglioni (ed), *Le calamità naturali nelle Alpi*. Istituto di Geografia dell'Università di Padova.

Vivian, R. (1976) *La Mer de Glace*. Fiches des glaciers français, Allier, Grenoble.

Vivian, R. (1977) Tourism, summer skiing, hydroelectricity and protection of the public in the French Alpine glacial area: the development of an applied glaciology, *Jour. Glaciology* **19**, 639–42.

Vivian, R. (1979) *Les glaciers sont vivants*. Denoël, Paris.

Walser, M. E. (1952) La crue de la Borgne le 4 août 1952, *Cours d'eau et énergie* **9**, 179–83.

Welsch, W. and Kinzl, H. (1970) Der Gletschersturz vom Huascaran (Peru) am 31. Mai 1970, die grösste Gletscherkatastrophe der Geschichte, *Zeitschrift für Gletscherkunde und Glazialgeologie* **6**, 181–92.

White, G. F. (ed.) (1974) *Natural hazards: local, national, global*. Oxford University Press, London and Toronto.

Winistorfer, J. (1977) Paléogéographie des stades glaciaires des vallées de la rive gauche du Rhône, entre Viège et Aproz (VS), *Bull. Murithienne* **94**, 3–65.

Worsley, P. and Alexander, M. J. (1976) Glacier and environmental changes – neoglacial data from the outermost moraine ridges, Northern Norway, *Geog. Annaler* **58A**, 55–69.

Zsigmondy, E. (1866) *Les dangers dans la montagne*. Attinger Frères, Neuchâtel.

INDEX